Norihiro Yagi won the 32nd Akatsuka Award for his debut work, *UNDEADMAN*, which appeared in *Monthly Shonen Jump* magazine and produced two sequels. His first serialized manga was his comedy *Angel Densetsu* (Angel Legend), which appeared in *Monthly Shonen Jump* from 1992 to 2000. His epic saga, *Claymore*, has been running in the magazine since 2001.

In his spare time, Yagi enjoys things like the Japanese comedic duo Downtown, martial arts, games, driving, and hard rock music, but he doesn't consider these actual hobbies.

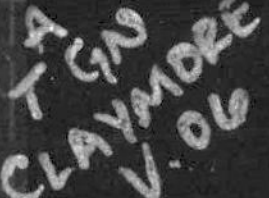

CLAYMORE VOL. 6
SHONEN JUMP ADVANCED Manga Edition

STORY AND ART BY
NORIHIRO YAGI

English Adaptation & Translation/Jonathan Tarbox
Touch-up Art & Lettering/Sabrina Heep
Design/Izumi Evers
Editor/Yuki Takagaki

Printed in the U.S.A.

Published by VIZ Media, LLC
P.O. Box 77010
San Francisco, CA 94107

10 9 8 7 6 5 4
First printing, February 2007
Fourth printing, August 2013

SHONEN JUMP ADVANCED Manga Edition

Claymore™

クレイモア

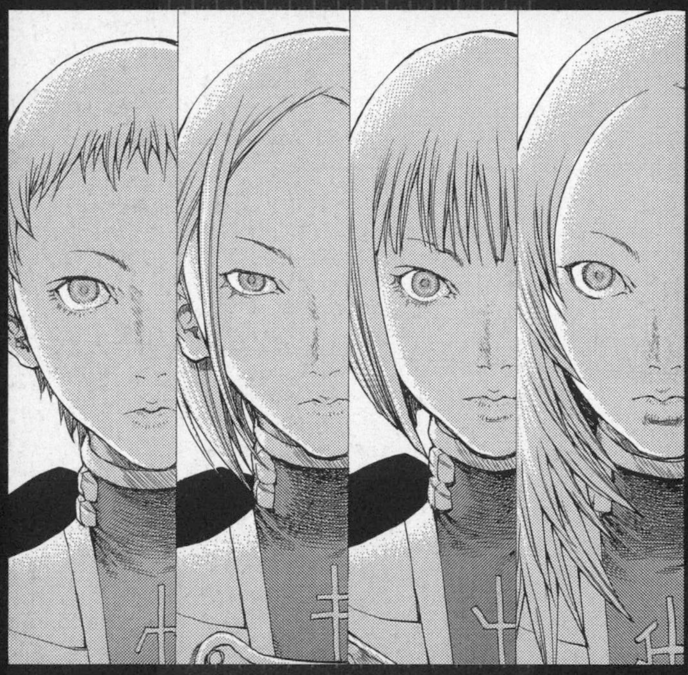

Vol. 6
The Endless Gravestones

Story and Art by Norihiro Yagi

broadswords that they carried.

Clare is assigned to a team that is hunting a "voracious eater." She and three other Claymores head off in pursuit, only to discover that their target is a monster far worse than they imagined. As the warriors fall one after the other, will they lose what hope they have left?

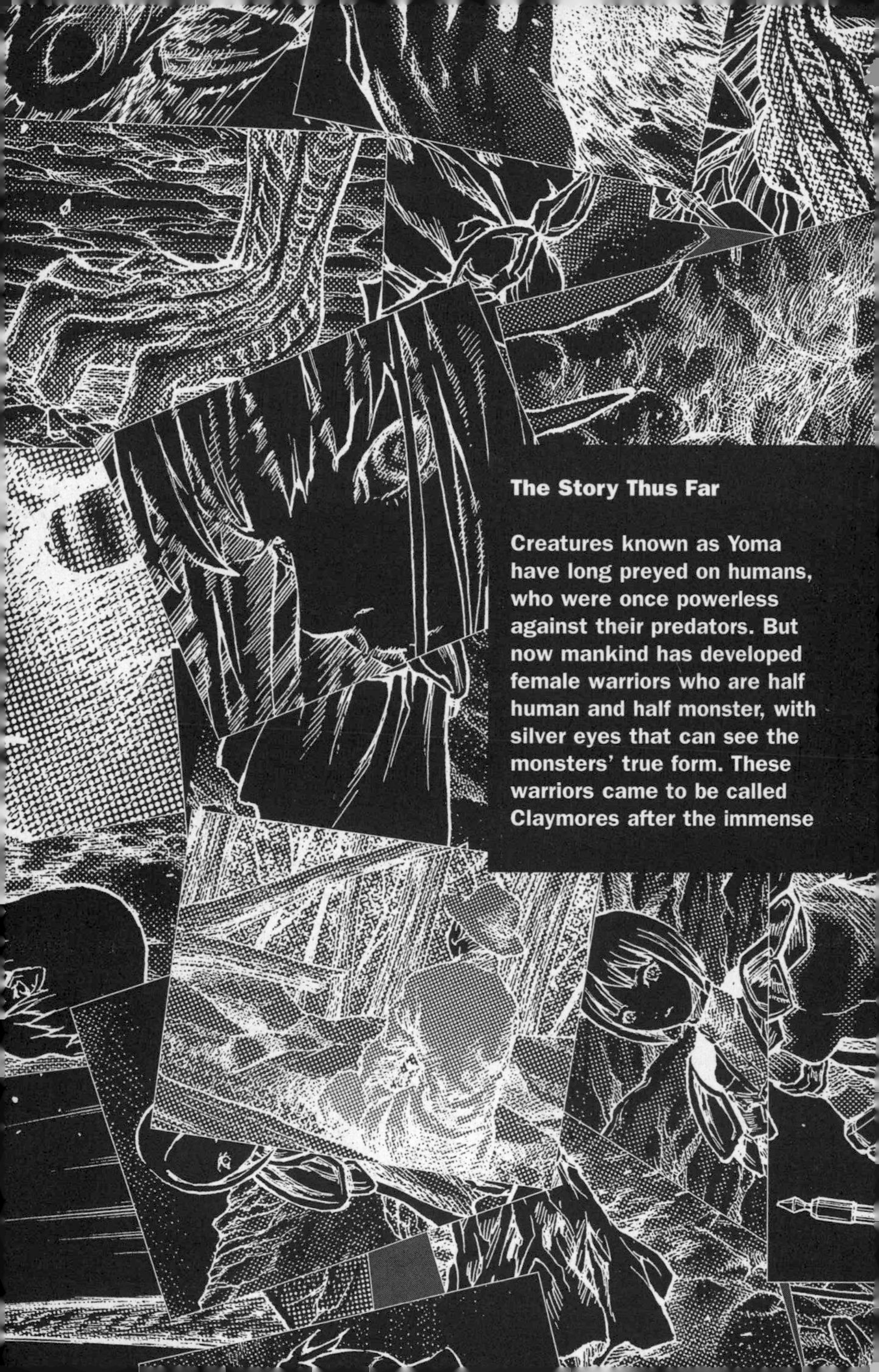

The Story Thus Far

Creatures known as Yoma have long preyed on humans, who were once powerless against their predators. But now mankind has developed female warriors who are half human and half monster, with silver eyes that can see the monsters' true form. These warriors came to be called Claymores after the immense

クレイモア

Claymore™

Vol. 6

CONTENTS

Scene 28: The Slashers, Part 4

SCENE 28:
THE SLASHERS, PART 4

TOO BAD, ISN'T IT?
I THINK YOU'VE MADE A FINE WARRIOR. YOU'RE SMART, WITH GOOD INSTINCTS.
FOR WARRIORS, IT'S NOT JUST ABOUT STRENGTH. THEY WON'T LIVE VERY LONG IF THEY'RE NOT SMART.

AND YET, IF THEY'RE TOO SMART ...
...THEY WON'T LIVE LONG, EITHER.
WHAT ...
...ARE YOU?

READ THIS WAY

LIKE YOU SAID ...
...THE REMAINS OF WHAT WAS ONCE A MALE WARRIOR.
NO MORE, NO LESS.

I DISPOSE OF THE WARRIORS SENT TO KILL ME TO STAY ALIVE.
THAT'S ALL.

BAM

!?

SHP

SHH

HUFF ...
HUFF ...
HUFF ...
BOKO
BOKO
BOKO
HER STOMACH HAS ALREADY STARTED TO HEAL.
BUT THE DAMAGE IS GREAT. THE CHANCES SHE'LL SURVIVE ARE FIFTY-FIFTY.

GRRR...
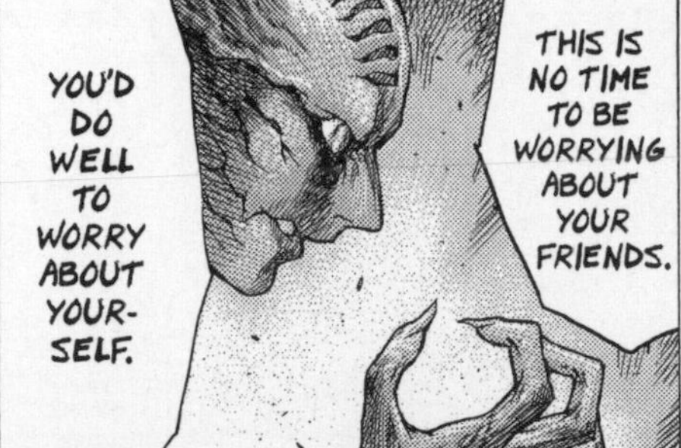
THIS IS NO TIME TO BE WORRYING ABOUT YOUR FRIENDS.
YOU'D DO WELL TO WORRY ABOUT YOURSELF.

GRAAAH!!
SHAA
BA

THOOK

DOGAGAGAGA

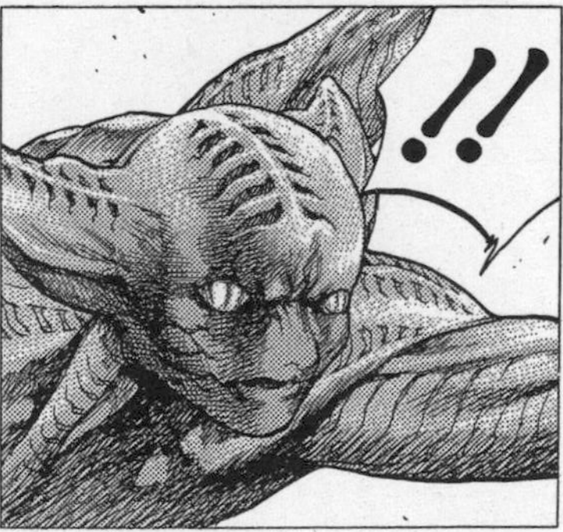

SHUP

UH ...
UGH ...

!?
SHE'S ...

GRAAAH!!
!

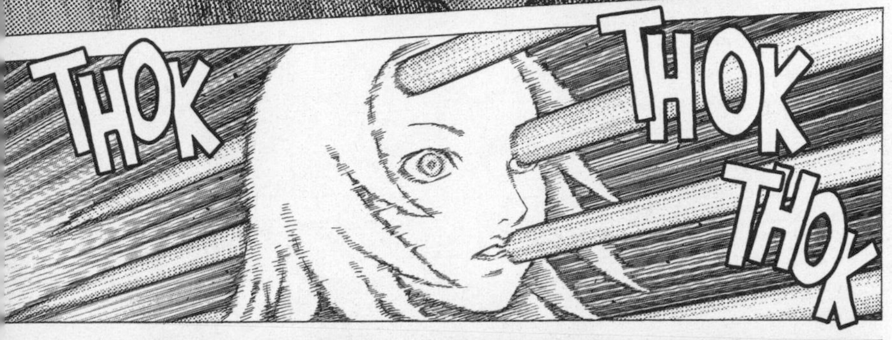

DOGAAAAAA

TMP

!!!

READ THIS WAY

THE WOUND ON HER BACK IS DEEP.
THIS ONE, TOO, HAS ONLY A FIFTY-FIFTY CHANCE.
IN ANY CASE ...
... THEY'RE IN NO CONDITION TO FIGHT.

HEH HEH HEH.
NOW I SEE.

FOR A BRIEF MOMENT, YOU CAN MOVE AT A FRIGHTENING SPEED.
IN THAT INSTANT, YOU'RE FASTER THAN ANY OTHER WARRIOR.

EVEN AMONG YOUR COMRADES, NOT ONE CAN MATCH YOUR SPEED.
YOU MUST BE A SINGLE DIGIT.

YOU MOVE LIKE A PHANTASM.
YOU MUST BE THE ONE CALLED ...

... PHAN-TOM MIRIA!
HOW FITTING.

READ
THIS
WAY

UGH ...
UGH ...

BUT I SENSE A WEAKNESS. YOU DON'T KEEP IT UP FOR LONG.
COULD THERE BE A REASON YOU'RE SO CAUTIOUS?

GISHI
BIKI
BIKI

LET'S SEE...
...IF YOUR TECHNIQUE WILL PREVAIL AGAINST ME.

DWOOM
BWA HA HA HA!
RUSHING TOWARD THE JAWS OF DEATH?
BIKI
VOOM

SHA
SHA
SHA
SHASH

!!!

THWOK

SHUP
GAH!
THOK
FWOOM
!!!
GAH!
THK
SHUP
UNH ...

!!
SHA
SHA
SHA
WHY ...
...YOU LITTLE...
SHUP
ZUSHAAAAT

KOFF ...
KOFF ...

SHE'S INCRED-IBLE.
DAMN IT!
IF SHE CAN DO THAT, WHY DIDN'T SHE DO IT BEFORE?
WE WOULDN'T BE IN...

IT'S PROBABLY A LAST RESORT.
SHE MUST NOT HAVE WANTED TO USE IT.
HUH?
IT'S A STRAIN FOR HER TO USE LARGE BURSTS OF YOMA POWER.
IT WOULD EXHAUST HER BODY AND MIND.

SHU
WU
SHU
WU
GA
SHUT
!!

I'LL BET MIRIA CAN DO IT ONLY A FEW TIMES.
MAYBE TEN...NO, 20 TIMES AT MOST.

BUT IT'S BEEN OVER 30 TIMES NOW.
SHE'S REALLY STRAIN-ING HER-SELF.
EH?
HOW DO YOU KNOW ALL THIS?
YOU'RE RANKED LOWEST OF US ALL.
WHAM
!

GOT YOU NOW!
SMIRK
AH...
AGH...
MIRIA!
AH...

YOU REALLY GAVE IT ALL YOU HAD.

BUT I KNEW IT COULDN'T LAST.

I HAD ONLY TO WAIT FOR YOU TO REACH YOUR LIMITS.

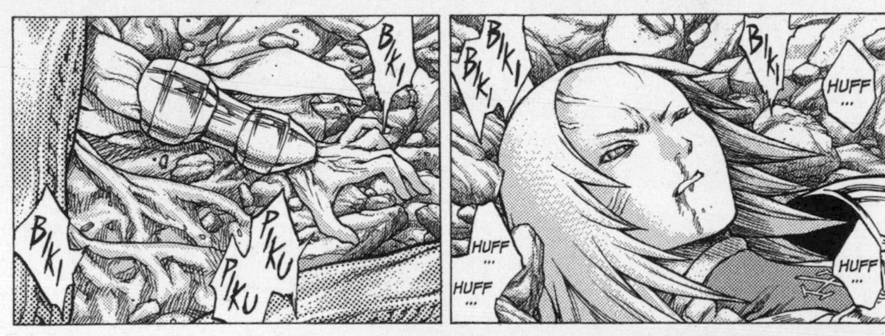

NOW, THEN ...
HOW SHALL I TORTURE YOU TO DEATH?

THOK

GAH!

GYAAAAH!!

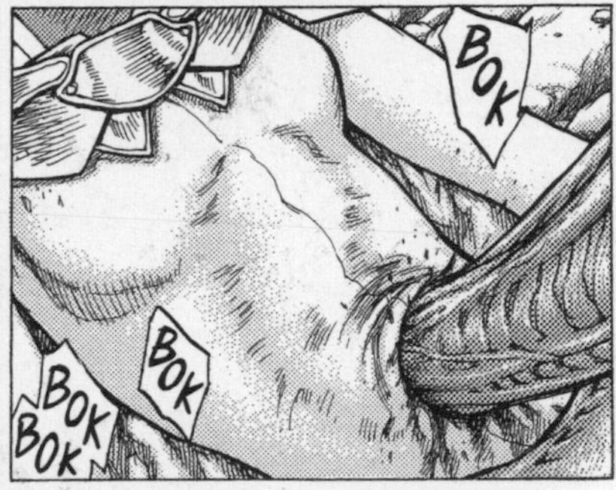

NO ...
DAMN IT!
!
DOSHA
UH...
DRIP DRIP
DRIP DRIP
UGH ...
DAMN IT!
I CAN'T ...
... MOVE ...
SHUDDER
SHUDDER
SHUDDER
SHUDDER

IT'S HOPE-LESS.

THIS IS THE END.

THERE'S NOTHING I CAN DO.

IT'S LIKE HE SAID. THIS IS TRUE DESPAIR.

BIKU

UH ...

BIKU

BIKU

GUH ...

CHP

DE-SPAIR?

AFTER ONLY THIS?

SHP

!

I'VE KNOWN A GREATER OPPO- NENT...

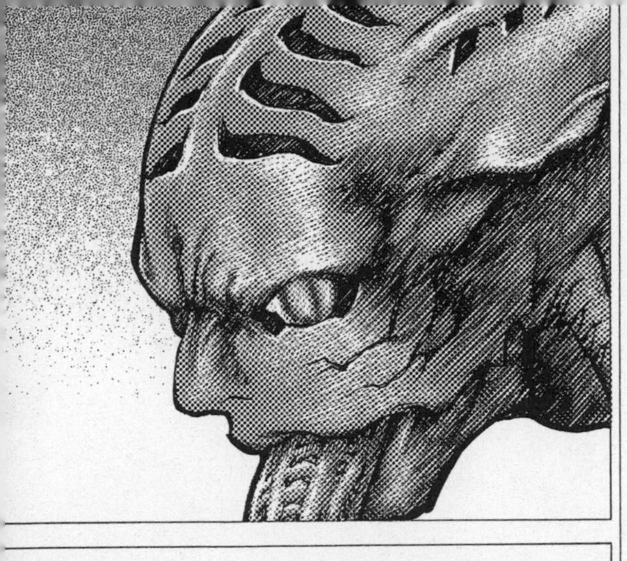

...AND FELT TRUE DESPAIR.

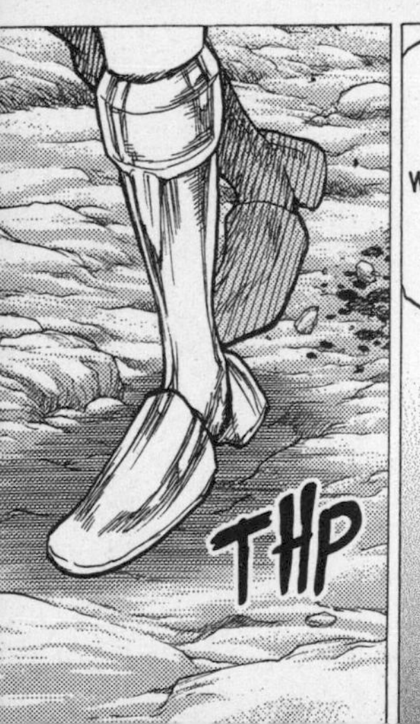
THP

BUT WHAT ABOUT ...
... YOUR WOUND?

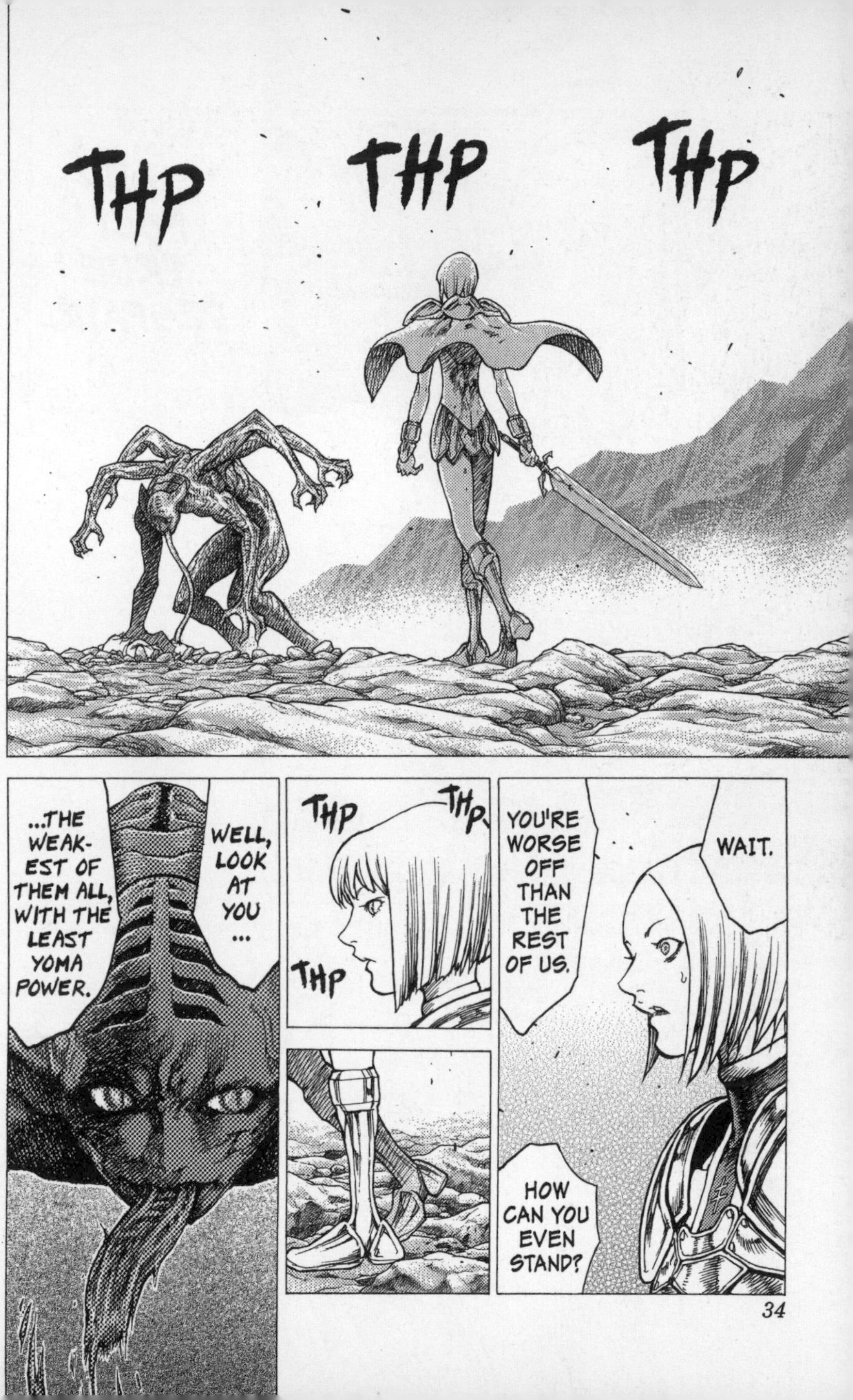

THP THP THP

WAIT.

YOU'RE WORSE OFF THAN THE REST OF US.

HOW CAN YOU EVEN STAND?

THP THP

THP

WELL, LOOK AT YOU ...

...THE WEAK-EST OF THEM ALL, WITH THE LEAST YOMA POWER.

READ THIS WAY

HAAA!

FWAT

DA GAGA GAT

ZUGAGAGAGAAA
GAGA
DOGA
WHAT ...?
WHY DO I KEEP MISS-ING?

READ THIS WAY

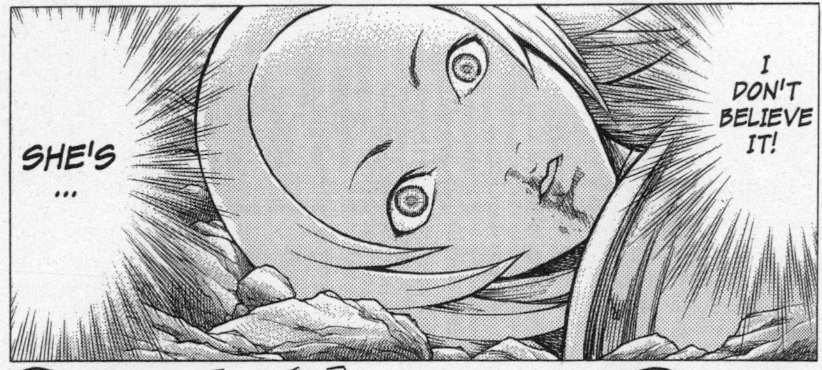
I DON'T BELIEVE IT!
SHE'S ...

DAGAGA
GA
DAGAGA

クレイモア
Claymore™

 SCENE 29: THE SLASHERS, PART 5

DOGAGAGA

SCENE 29: THE SLASHERS, PART 5

GAGA

DOGA

READ THIS WAY

KEEP CALM.
SUPPRESS EVERY OUNCE OF MY YOMA POWER...

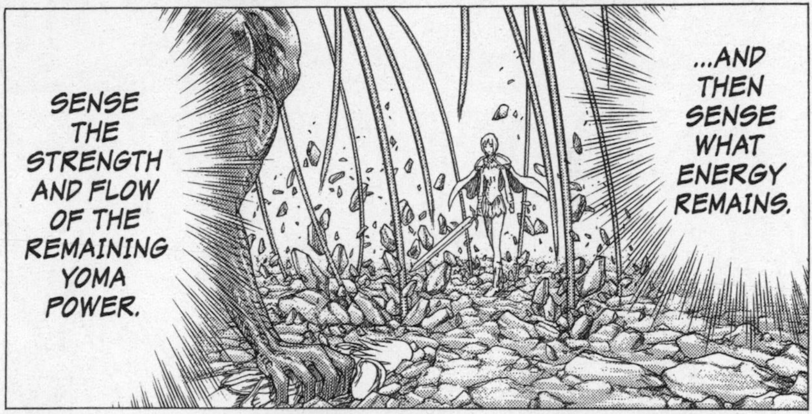
SENSE THE STRENGTH AND FLOW OF THE REMAINING YOMA POWER.
...AND THEN SENSE WHAT ENERGY REMAINS.

IGNORE WHAT MY EYES SEE.
I MUST GRASP THE FLOW OF THE YOMA POWER...
...AND FROM THE SIZE AND FLOW, PREDICT THE PATH OF ATTACK.
AND THEN...

SHUBA
DOGAAAAT
SHE'S EVAD-ING HIM!
BY THE TIME HE ATTACKS, SHE'S DODGED HIM!
!

DOGAGAGA

DOGA
GAGA

SO... THAT'S WHAT FELT WRONG WHEN I FOUGHT HER.
I SEE IT NOW!

SHE WASN'T WATCHING ME, SHE WAS WATCHING THE FLOW OF MY YOMA ENERGY.
EVEN WHILE WE WERE BOTH SUPPRES-SING OUR YOMA ENERGY, SHE WAS STILL TRYING TO READ THE FLOW.

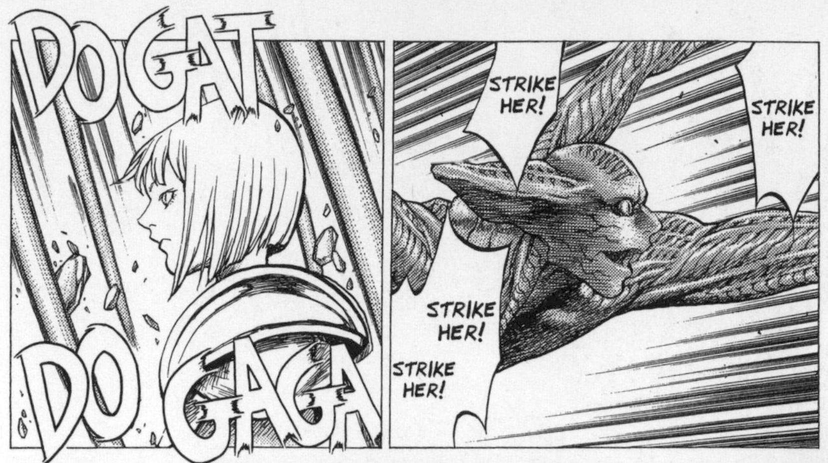
STRIKE HER!
STRIKE HER!
STRIKE HER!
STRIKE HER!
DOGAT
DO GAGA

THAT MEANS, THE STRONGER HER OPPONENT'S YOMA POWER, THE EASIER IT IS FOR HER TO SENSE IT.
IT'S THE PERFECT WAY TO FIGHT AN AWAKENED BEING, WHICH RELEASES HUGE AMOUNTS OF ENERGY.

GAAH!!

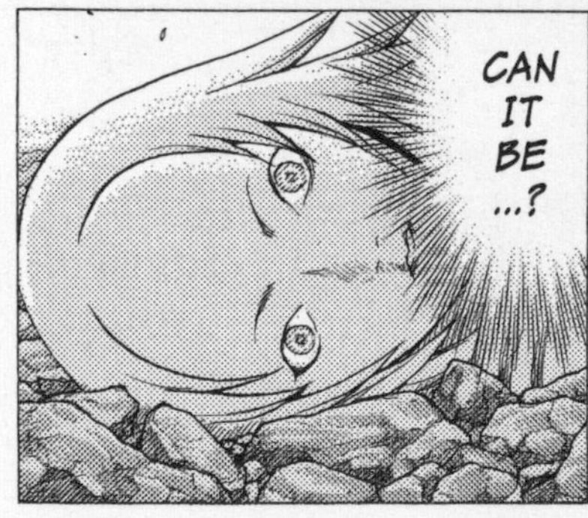
CAN IT BE ...?

!!!

DID SHE SINGLE-MINDEDLY PRACTICE THIS MOVE...
...FOR THE SOLE PURPOSE OF FIGHTING AN AWAKENED BEING?

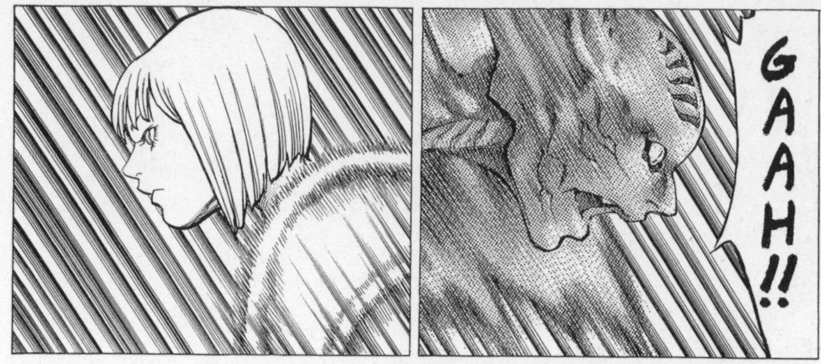
GAAH!!

WAH
AK

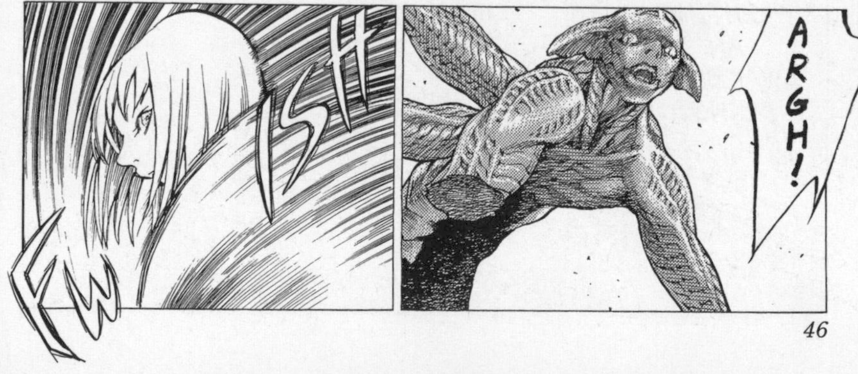
ARGH!
FWISH

SHUP
FWOSH

GRAAH!

GRIP

SHAA
GYUT
BABAT

FWAK
THOK
WHAK
WAKACH
!
CHUN

GASHA
ZU BA A A
THP!
THK
SHUUM
!!

GAH
...

ZA SHAAAA

READ THIS WAY

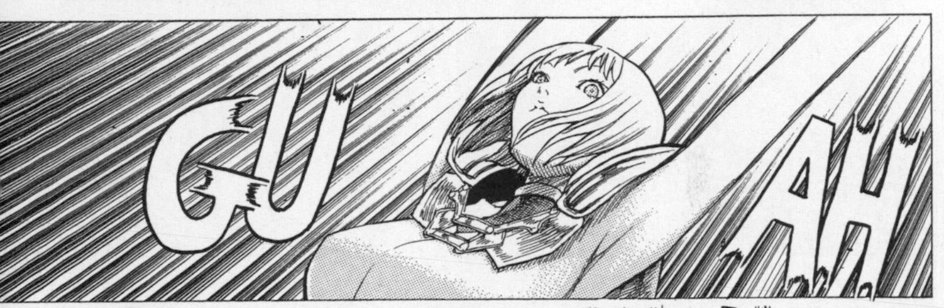

WHAAAM

GAH

UGH ...

THROB THROB

DOGA
A
T
WHAM
I CAN'T TELL IF YOU'RE STRONG OR WEAK.
WHAT IS IT WITH YOU?
!?
GAK!
HAH!

IN SHORT...
...YOU NEED MORE PRAC-TICE.
MIRIA!

!!

W...

WAIT, PLEASE!
I HAVE SOMETHING TO TELL YOU!
YOU SEE ...

WATCH OUT...
... BELOW YOU.

EVEN IN THIS CONDITION...
...I'M STILL A SINGLE DIGIT.

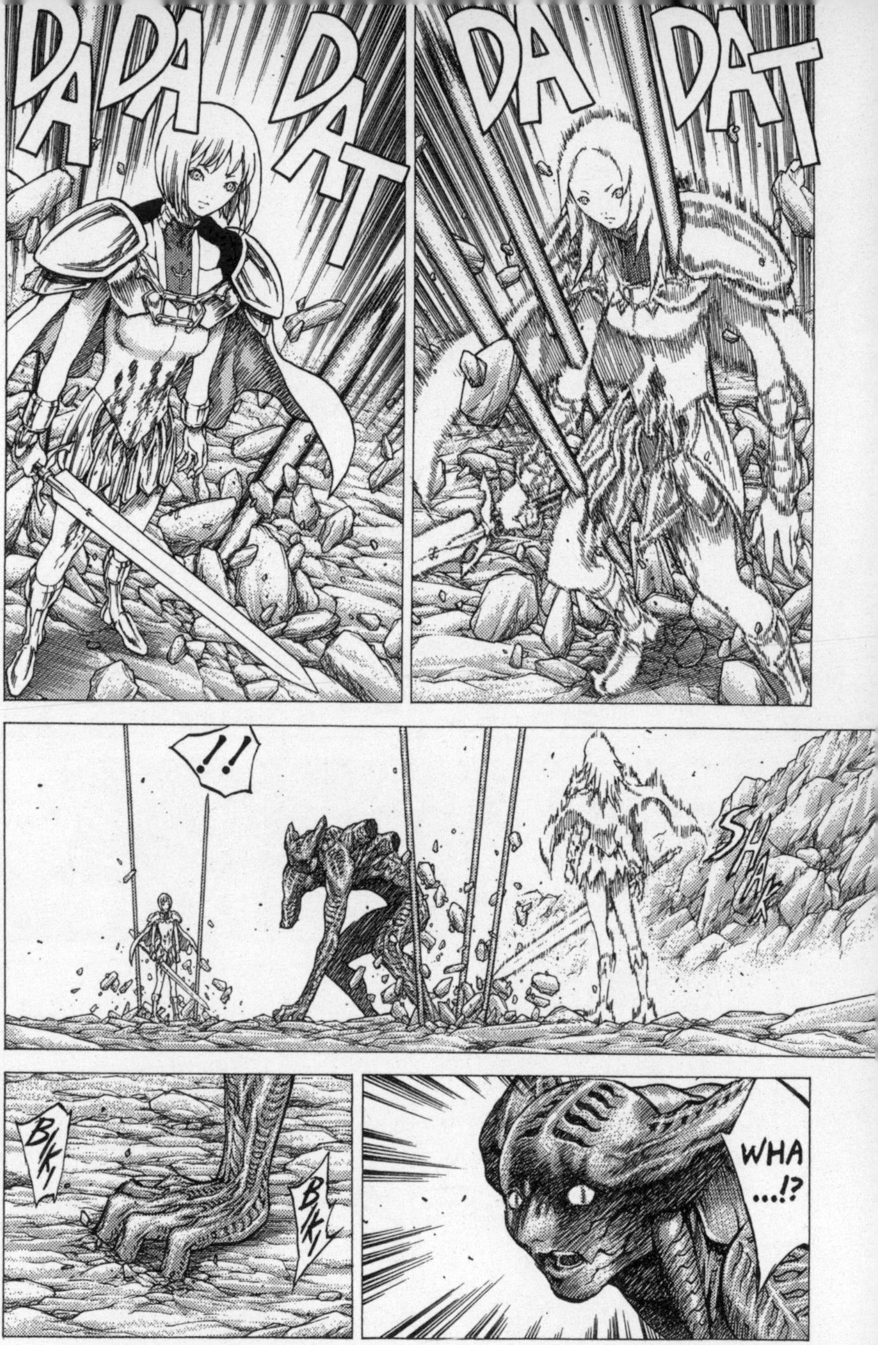

DADA DAT
DA DAT

!!
SHAK

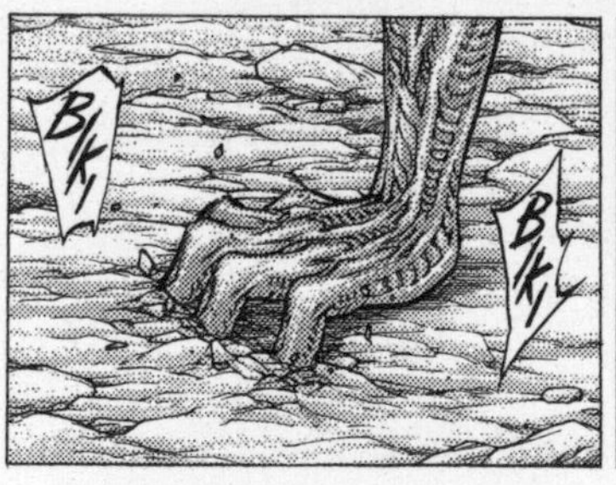
BIKI
BIKI

WHA ...!?

READ
THIS
WAY

THERE ARE SO MANY THINGS I WANT TO ASK.
SH AK
BUT SINCE YOU WON'T TELL US...

SHAK

LET'S GO!
AND DON'T FALL BEHIND!

YOU EITHER!

GRAI!
AAH!

GU
AAH
DA
GAGA
THOK

BWA
ASH

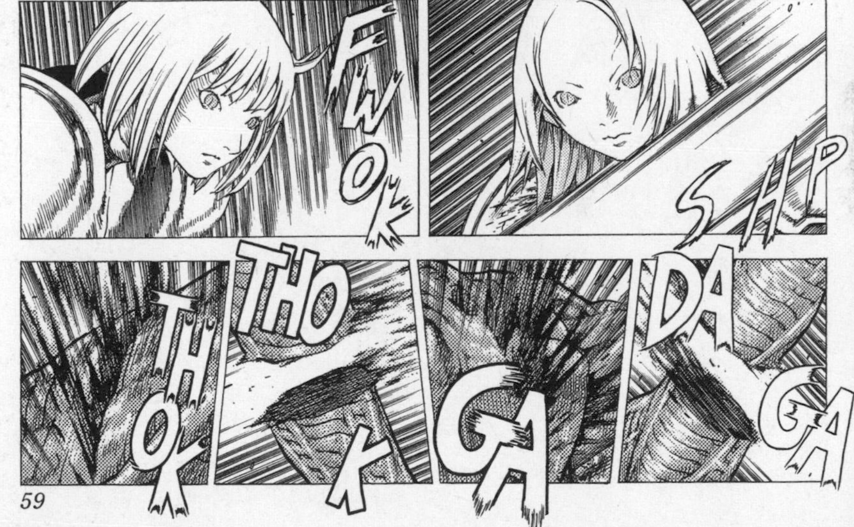

NO...
IT CAN'T BE!

NOT TO THESE TWO...
NOT ME!

D...
DAMN IT!

DOSHAAAT

YOU ...

YOU DID IT.

SHIVER

AH ...

THUD

!

HMM ...

I'M A MESS.

HOW IS SHE?
NOT GOOD. SHE USED ALL HER YOMA POWER TO REGENERATE HER ARM, SO HER STOMACH WOUND ISN'T HEALING.
IT ALL DEPENDS ON HER OWN STRENGTH NOW.

SO, WHY AREN'T *YOU* HURT WORSE?
!
YOU TOOK MORE BLOWS THAN WE DID.

HER VITAL ORGANS ARE INTACT.
!
WITH A LITTLE TIME, HER WOUNDS SHOULD HEAL.

HMPH...

READ THIS WAY

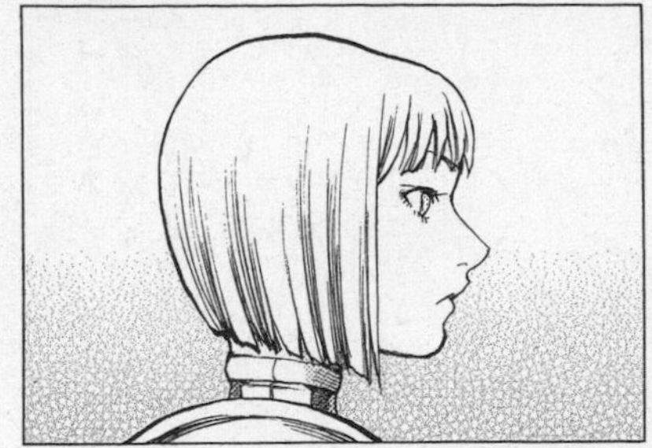

AND NOW, THERE'S SOMETHING I NEED TO ASK YOU BOTH.
UP
SHU
IT'S EXTREMELY IMPORTANT TO ALL OF US, SO I NEED YOU TO ANSWER AS HONESTLY AS POS-SIBLE.

OH?

HAS THERE EVER BEEN A TIME...
...WHEN EITHER OF YOU HAVE ALMOST AWAKENED?

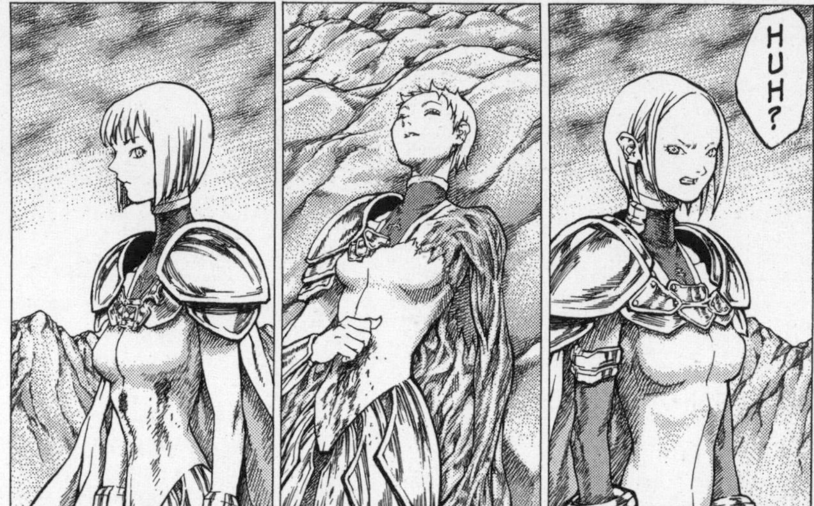
HUH?

YES.
!
A WHILE AGO, WHEN I FOUGHT IN RABONA CATHEDRAL, I EXHAUSTED MY STRENGTH AND MADE THE MISTAKE OF FORCING MY YOMA POWER TO ITS LIMITS.

I FELT A RUSH OF SUFFER-ING AND ECSTASY.
SOME-HOW I WAS ABLE TO PULL MYSELF BACK.

READ THIS WAY

OH...
SAME WITH ME.
I GOT CARRIED AWAY AND LOST CON-TROL.
THE IMPULSE TO AWAKEN WAS TOO STRONG, JUST LIKE IT WAS FOR THE MALES.
BUT I WAS ABLE TO TURN BACK AND SUPPRESS IT.

IT HAPPENED TO DENEVE, TOO. SHE TOLD ME ABOUT IT.
IT WAS WHEN SHE WAS TRYING TO DISCOVER HER LIMITS.

WHEN WAS THAT?
ABOUT THE SAME TIME AS ME.

THEN TELL ME THIS...
HAVE EITHER OF YOU CAUSED PROBLEMS FOR A CLIENT OR FOR ORDINARY FOLK?
!

I HAVE, A FEW TIMES.
BECAUSE OF THE CODE I'VE NEVER TAKEN A LIFE, BUT I'VE COME CLOSE TO IT.
FOR DENEVE, IT WASN'T OTHER PEOPLE. SHE'S MORE THE TYPE TO STIR UP TROUBLE AGAINST HER OWN KIND.

I SEE.
AND THAT LEAVES A LOW-RANKING WARRIOR WHO DISOBEYS ORDERS AND RUNS WILD FROM TIME TO TIME.
THE WARRIORS WHO ARE GATHERED HERE ARE TROUBLE-MAKERS WHO'VE COME CLOSE TO AWAKEN-ING.

HUH!?

I DON'T GET IT. ARE YOU SAYING THERE'S SOME-THING BEHIND THIS JOB?

THIS IS ONLY SPECU-LATION...
...BUT IT'S MY THEORY THAT WE'RE PROBLEM CASES WHO WERE SENT TO FIGHT AN AWAKENED BEING THAT WE WERE NO MATCH FOR.

HOW DO YOU FIT IN?
YOU DON'T LOOK LIKE AN AWAKENED BEING, OR EVEN A PROBLEM CASE.
!

READ THIS WAY

I NEARLY AWAK-ENED, TOO.
ON MY THIRD HUNT FOR AN AWAKENED BEING, I REALIZED THAT I WAS HUNTING AN OLD FRIEND.

I HACKED OFF ITS ARMS AND LEGS AND WAS ABOUT TO PUSH THE BLADE INTO ITS THROAT WHEN I REALIZED IT WAS HER.
UNTIL THAT MOMENT, SHE HADN'T SAID A WORD, CALLED MY NAME, OR REVERTED TO HER ORIGINAL FORM AND SHOWED ME HER FACE.

FROM THAT DAY ON...
...I SWORE TO TAKE REVENGE ON THE PEOPLE WHO MADE ME WHAT I AM.

Scene 30: The Slashers, Part 6

READ THIS WAY

BLORP

WHY?

WHY DIDN'T YOU CALL MY NAME?

WHY DIDN'T YOU SHOW ME IT WAS YOU?

WHY?

WHY?

SHE NO LONGER HAD A HUMAN CONSCIOUSNESS.

DON'T THINK ON IT TOO DEEPLY.

AFTER ALL...

...IT WAS A YOMA.

GO WAHH

READ THIS WAY
INTER-ESTING.
IT'S PHANTOM MIRIA. I HEAR SHE FIGHTS EVEN BETTER IN A GROUP THAN NO. 1.
IF SHE AWAKENS, I'D *LOVE* TO FIGHT HER.
HUH?
GA!
GA!
GA!
GA!
GA!
GA!
BIKI
BIKI
BIKI
GA!
GA!
GA!
GA!
GA!
GA!
GA!
GA!
GA!
GA!
GA!
GA!
GA!

READ THIS WAY

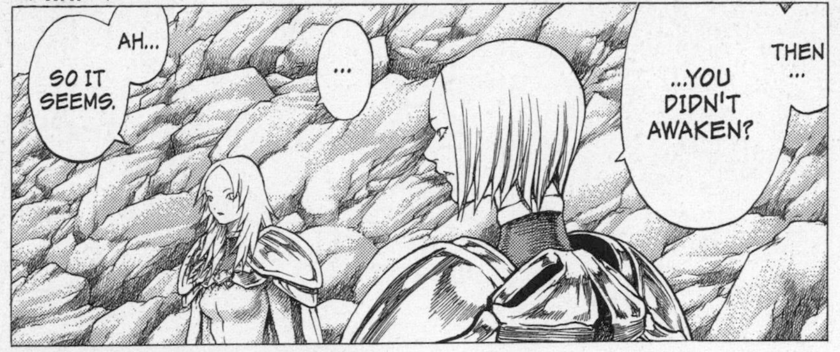
THEN ...
...YOU DIDN'T AWAKEN?
...
AH...
SO IT SEEMS.

I KNEW I'D LOST CONTROL OF MY YOMA POWER, BUT I TRIED MY BEST TO SUPPRESS IT.
I THINK I ALSO HATED KNOWING THAT SHE WAS THE ONE WHO'D PUSHED ME TO THAT POINT.
SHE ...?
UH...
AS I WAS SAYING...

...AFTER THAT, I PLOTTED MY REVENGE AGAINST THE ORGANIZATION.
I WON'T FORGIVE THEM FOR WHAT THEY DID TO MY BODY, OR FOR TREATING US LIKE WE'RE EXPENDABLE.

I DID MY BEST TO LOOK DUTIFUL, BUT I WAS INVESTIGATING THE ORGANIZATION IN SECRET.
I WAS LOOKING FOR A WEAKNESS.

AND THAT'S HOW...
...I LEARNED THE ORGANI-ZATION'S GREATEST SECRET.

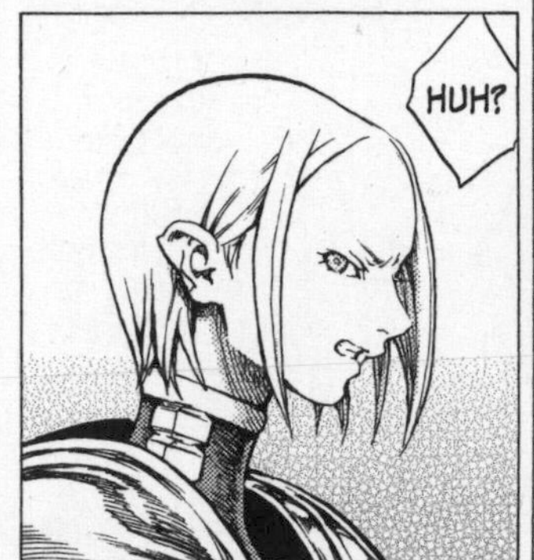
HUH?

WHAT DO YOU MEAN, "ITS GREATEST SECRET"?

SOME THINGS ARE BETTER LEFT UNSAID.
IF I TOLD YOU, THERE'D BE NO TURNING BACK.

READ THIS WAY

HMPH...
HOW POM-POUS!

SO YOU LEARNED SOMETHING THAT THE ORGANI-ZATION WANTS TO HIDE, AND NOW THEY'RE TRYING TO GET RID OF YOU?
!

LIKE I SAID, IT'S ONLY SPECU-LATION.
BUT WE ALL HAVE ONE THING IN COMMON.

I HAVE ...
...ONE MORE THING TO ASK YOU.

HAS ANY-THING ...

... CHANGED IN US SINCE WE CAME SO CLOSE TO AWAK-ENING?

!

EACH OF YOU MUST HAVE FELT SOMETHING.
BEFORE AWAKENING AND AFTER, THE QUALITY OF OUR YOMA POWER IS CLEARLY DIFFERENT.
IT ISN'T LIMITED THE WAY IT WAS BEFORE.
AND NOW AND THEN, YOU FEEL PANGS OF HUNGER.

WE FOUR ...
... HAVE ALREADY AWAK-ENED.

WELL?
WHAT DO YOU SENSE?

ONE HAS STRONG YOMA ENERGY.
ONE IS AVER-AGE.
ONE IS WEAK.
AND THE LAST ONE I CAN'T TELL. SHE COULD BE DEAD.
EVEN IF SHE'S STILL ALIVE, SHE'S VERY WEAK.
I DON'T SENSE AN AWAKENED BEING.

IF I MOVED CLOSER...
...I THINK I COULD BE MORE CERTAIN.
ANY CLOSER, AND THEY'D NOTICE YOU.
YOU'RE THE ONLY ONE WHO CAN SENSE YOMA ENERGY FROM THIS DISTANCE. THAT'S WHY WE CALLED YOU IN.

READ THIS WAY

WHAT IS THIS ABOUT?
WHAT COULD BE SO IMPORTANT ABOUT THE FATE OF A FEW WARRIORS HUNTING AN AWAKENED BEING?
THINK OF IT AS THE CONCERN OF A PARENT FOR A CHILD.
DON'T FRET ABOUT IT.

!
!?
WHAT IS IT?

YOMA POWER.

SUR-PRISE AND UNEASE.
THE STRONG ONE...
...JUST SAID SOME-THING THAT MADE THE OTHER TWO UNEASY.

ESPECIALLY THE AVERAGE ONE.

SHE'S ARGUING, GESTURING WITH HER HANDS AND BODY.

SHE SEEMS THE PASSIONATE TYPE.

THE WEAK ONE IS LISTENING CALMLY.

READ THIS WAY

SHE'S GOOD ...
... SENSING ALL THAT FROM HERE.

!
THE LAST ONE HAS REGAINED CONSCIOUS-NESS.
!

GOOD.
ALL FOUR WILL COME BACK ALIVE.

I SEE.
IN THAT CASE ...
...MEMO-RIZE THEIR AURAS.
ZAT

BECAUSE...
...SOME-DAY YOU MAY HAVE TO CROSS SWORDS WITH THEM.

YOU'RE NOT SERIOUS!

DON'T LUMP ME TOGETHER WITH THOSE MON-STERS!
WE AREN'T LIKE THAT!
I HAVE NO DESIRE TO EAT HUMAN INTES-TINES!

LET ME EXPLAIN.
IT'S NOT THAT WE'VE FULLY AWAKENED. RATHER, WE'RE IN A HALF-AWAKENED STATE.
MOST FULLY AWAKEN IN ONE STEP, BUT WE'VE STOPPED JUST SHORT OF THAT FOR SOME REASON.
OR WE MAY GRADU-ALLY AWAKEN.

READ THIS WAY

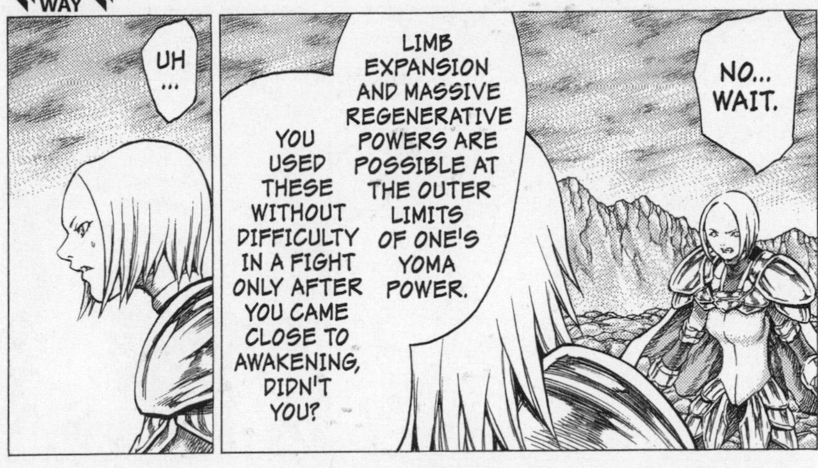
NO... WAIT.
LIMB EXPANSION AND MASSIVE REGENERATIVE POWERS ARE POSSIBLE AT THE OUTER LIMITS OF ONE'S YOMA POWER.
YOU USED THESE WITHOUT DIFFICULTY IN A FIGHT ONLY AFTER YOU CAME CLOSE TO AWAKENING, DIDN'T YOU?
UH ...

AFTER YOU'VE CROSSED OVER, RETURNING TO NORMAL ...
... SHOULD BE IMPOS-SIBLE!

WHA ...?

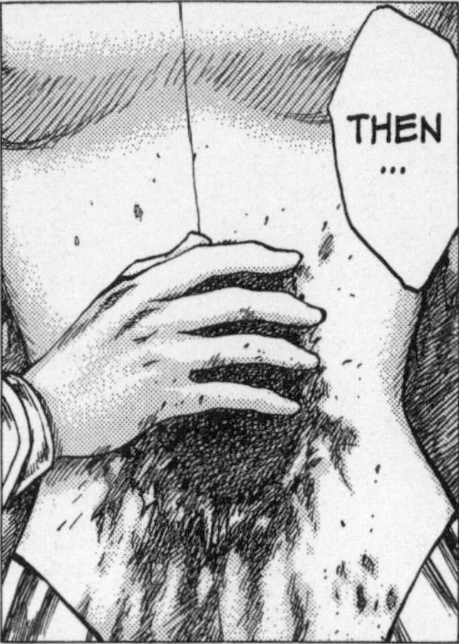
THEN ...

THEN ...
WHAT WILL HAPPEN TO US?
!

ARE WE JUST GOING TO...
...SIT BACK AND WATCH OUR-SELVES AWAKEN?

DENEVE!

I'M SORRY, THAT'S ALL I KNOW.
WE MAY HAVE AVOIDED AWAKENING ALTOGETHER, OR WE COULD BE SLOWLY MOVING TOWARD IT.

READ THIS WAY

EITHER WAY...
...WE WON'T KNOW WHERE OR WHEN WE COULD AWAKEN. ALL WE KNOW IS THAT THE SITUATION IS PRECARIOUS.

ALL RIGHT.
THEN I'LL BE THE TEST CASE.
!
WATCH CLOSELY.

WATCH WHAT?

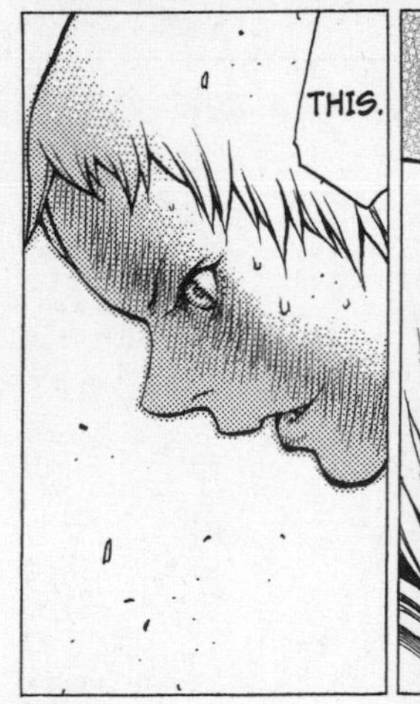
THIS.

BWOOM

READ THIS WAY

STOP IT, DENEVE!
IF YOU FORCE YOUR YOMA POWER IN YOUR CONDITION...

SHUT UP AND WATCH!
IF I DON'T FORCE IT AND TRY TO REGENERATE, I'LL DIE ANYWAY.
LET'S SEE IF I CAN RELEASE MY YOMA POWER ALL AT ONCE.

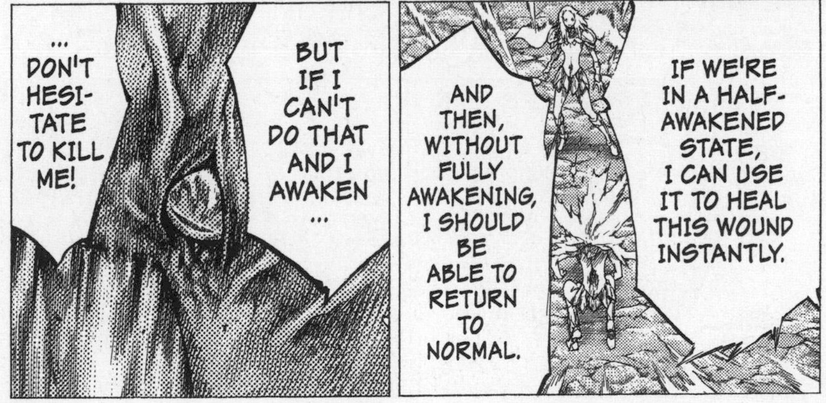
IF WE'RE IN A HALF-AWAKENED STATE, I CAN USE IT TO HEAL THIS WOUND INSTANTLY.
AND THEN, WITHOUT FULLY AWAKENING, I SHOULD BE ABLE TO RETURN TO NORMAL.
BUT IF I CAN'T DO THAT AND I AWAKEN ...
... DON'T HESITATE TO KILL ME!

GASHAN
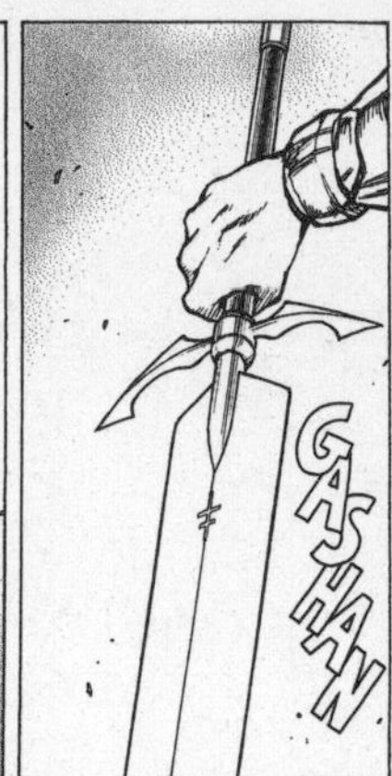
GASHAN

DENE
...

!
HELEN.
CLARE.
GASH AN

RIGHT.
WE WON'T FAIL YOU.

DENEVE, YOU'RE AN OLD FRIEND.
WE WON'T LET YOU SUFFER.

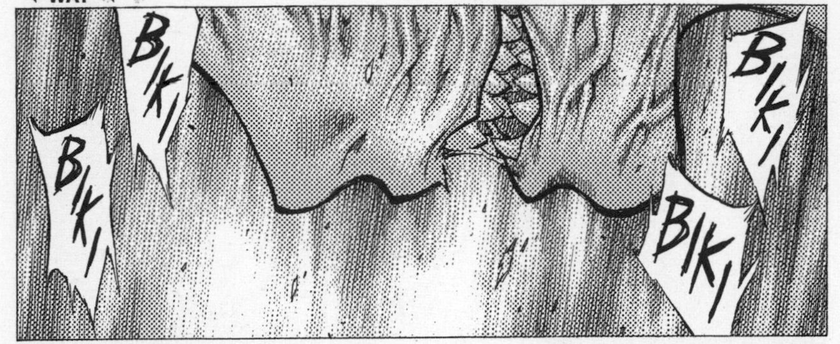

DOGA

AAAAA

WHAT IS IT?
HAS SOMETHING HAPPENED?

ONE OF THE FOUR HAS AWAKENED.
WHAT?
IT APPEARS SHE WENT BEYOND HER LIMITS AND AWAKENED OF HER OWN FREE WILL.
BUT WHY?

READ THIS WAY

PERHAPS SHE'S INJURED, AND MISJUDGED HER LIMITS.
TURN
A PITY.

AND THAT'S ALL?
YOU SAID THEY WERE LIKE YOUR OWN CHILD-REN.
I DON'T RECALL MAKING A MONSTER MY CHILD.

READ
THIS
WAY

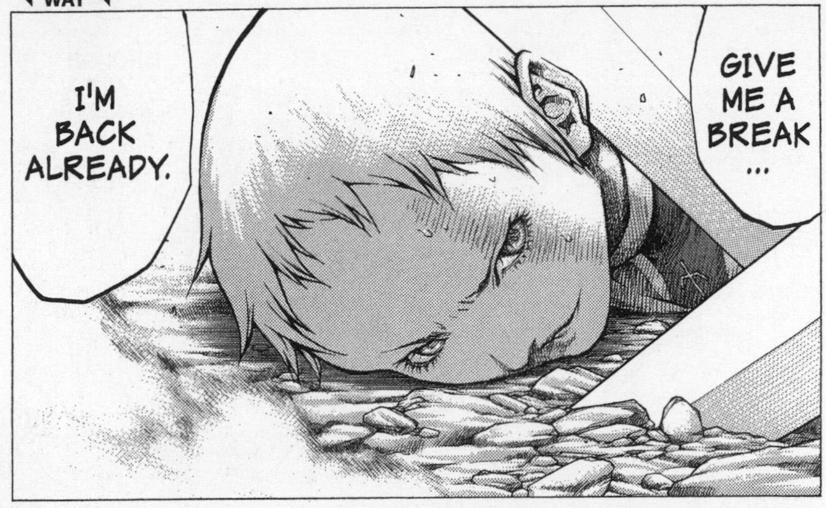
GIVE ME A BREAK ...
I'M BACK ALREADY.

DENEVE!

WHEW

HMPH ...
THAT WAS CLOSE.

IS YOUR STOMACH ALL RIGHT?
YES.
THE WOUND FINALLY CLOSED.

ENOUGH OF THIS MADNESS.
YOU CAME BACK, BUT YOU MAY NOT BE SO LUCKY NEXT TIME.

THERE'S TOO MUCH WE DON'T KNOW.
IF YOU WANT TO KEEP YOUR HUMAN CONSCIOUSNESS, YOU'D BETTER NOT BE SO RECKLESS.

I KNOW.
I COULD LIVE WITHOUT ANOTHER RISK LIKE THAT.
GASHAK

KACHAN

READ
THIS
WAY

BASHA

?
WHAT IS IT, CLARE?

I THINK...
...WE'RE BEING WATCHED.
DON'T WORRY. I'VE CHECKED THE AREA.
I DON'T SENSE OUR COMRADES' AURAS FROM HERE TO THE MOUNTAINS.
AND EVEN IF SOMEONE WERE BEYOND THAT...
...THEY COULDN'T KNOW WE WERE HERE.

AH...

SO SHE COULD SENSE ME FROM THAT FAR.
BUT SHE'S NOT SURE, IT SEEMS.

IN ANY CASE, WHAT WAS THAT ALL ABOUT?
THE ONE I THOUGHT WAS AWAKENED HAS CALMED DOWN.

THAT'S HARD TO BELIEVE.
IS SUCH A THING POSSIBLE?

READ THIS WAY

HEY, WHAT'S WRONG?
DID SOME-THING ELSE HAPPEN?

I THINK I WAS MISTAKEN ABOUT THE AWAKEN-ING.
ALL FOUR ARE NORMAL.

YOU? WRONG?
THAT'S UNUSUAL.

LIKE I SAID... WE'RE TOO FAR AWAY.
IT'S DIFFICULT TO GET A CLEAR READING FROM THIS DISTANCE.

BUT I SUPPOSE YOUR PARENTAL CONCERN ...
...HAS ITS LIMITS, TOO.

COME.
LET'S GO, GALATEA.
SHP

HMPH.

HE MAY BE A PARENT...
...BUT HE'S STILL A WILY FOX.

SHAK

WE'LL CROSS SWORDS SOME DAY...
...PER-HAPS.

READ THIS WAY

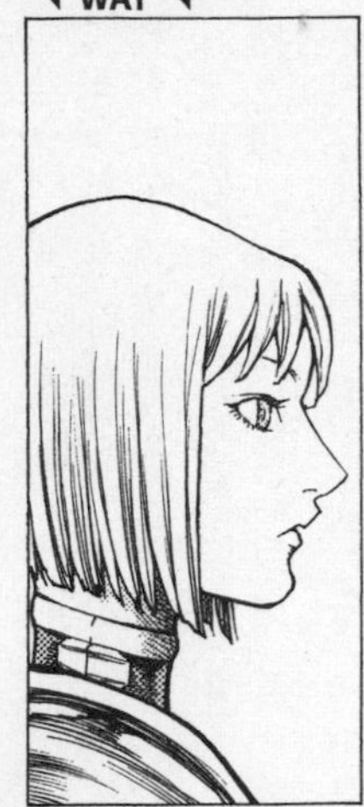

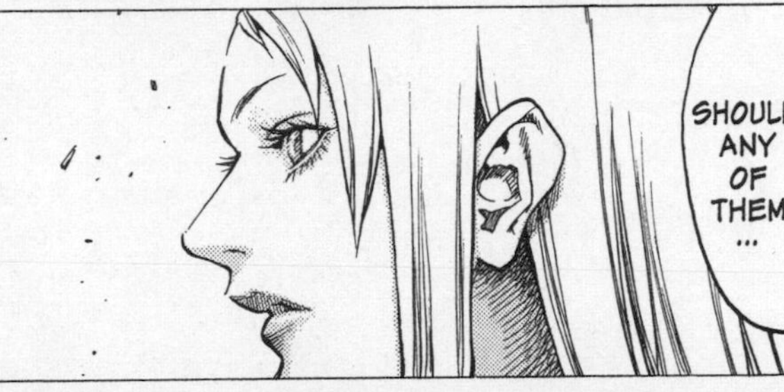
SHOULD ANY OF THEM ...
...SURVIVE LONG ENOUGH TO MEET ME...

...IT WILL BE...
...A LONG AND THORNY ROAD.

クレイモア
Claymore™

Scene 31: The Endless Gravestones, Part 1

SHH
ZU BA
ZU BA
SHUUN
!!
DASH
T

ZUBAAA
SCENE 31: THE ENDLESS GRAVESTONES, PART 1

IN... CREDIBLE.
SO THAT'S A SILVER-EYED WITCH.
SHE KILLED THREE YOMA AT ONCE.

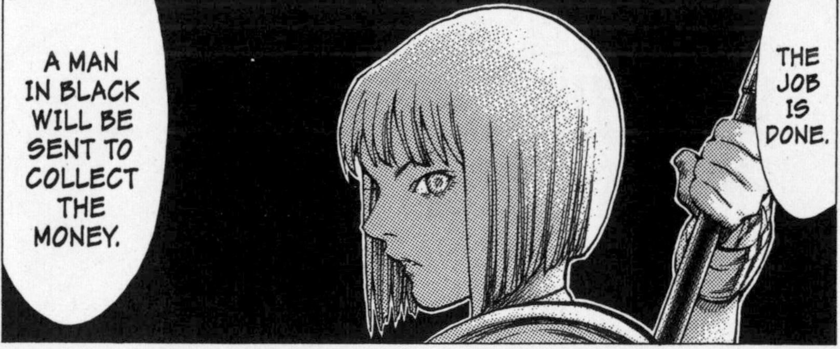

READ THIS WAY

CLARE, YOU'VE BEEN AMAZING LATELY.
YOU CAN STRIKE DOWN THREE OR FOUR YOMA AT ONCE.

IT'S GOTTEN SO THAT IN BATTLE, I CAN READ THE ENERGY OF ORDINARY YOMA AND AWAKENED BEINGS.
I CAN BEAT THEM, NO MATTER HOW MANY THERE ARE.
GRIP

BUT IF I WANT TO STAY ALIVE...
...I HAVE TO GET STRONGER.

WE'LL PART WAYS NOW.

GO BACK TO YOUR REGIONS AND YOUR POSTS.
WE MAY HAVE BEEN MISINFORMED ABOUT THE JOB, BUT WE CARRIED IT OUT.
THAT'S ALL WE DID.

READ THIS WAY

IT WOULD BE TOO RISKY TO JOIN FORCES NOW AGAINST THE ORGANIZATION.
WE KNOW NOTHING AND SUSPECT NOTHING... WE FINISHED OUR JOB AND WENT HOME.
THAT'S WHAT WE WANT THEM TO THINK.

BUT DON'T LET DOWN YOUR GUARD, EVEN FOR A MOMENT. BE CAREFUL WITH EVERY STEP YOU TAKE.
MEANWHILE, FOLLOW ORDERS AND KEEP A LOW PROFILE. TRY TO STAMP OUT YOUR IMAGE AS TROUBLE-MAKERS.
THEY'RE IN NO HURRY TO GET RID OF US, SO WE SHOULD GET AWAY WITH THIS FOR A WHILE.

EXCEPT FOR ME.

BUT ...
...WHAT WILL YOU DO NOW, MIRIA?

OUR AWAKENING DOESN'T LEAVE US MUCH TIME, SO I'LL LET YOU KNOW AS SOON AS I'VE FOUND SOMETHING.
DON'T DO ANYTHING UNTIL YOU HEAR FROM ME.

I'M PAST THE POINT OF NO RETURN.
I'LL KEEP INVESTI-GATING THE ORGANI-ZATION.

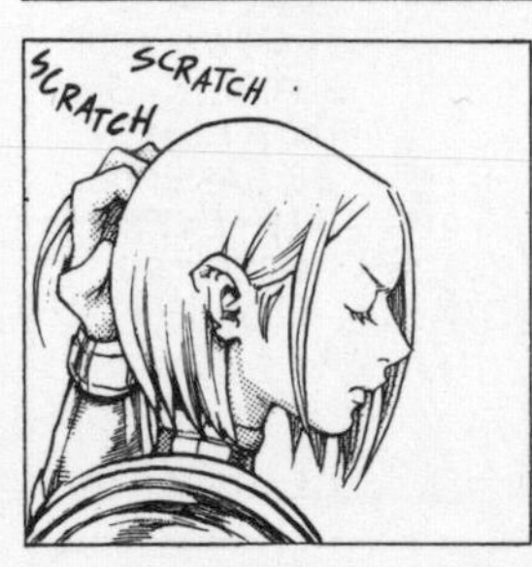
SCRATCH
SCRATCH

...

DON'T WORRY. YOUR POWERS HAVE GROWN SINCE YOU ALMOST AWAKENED.
YOU'D RIVAL ANY SINGLE DIGIT.
IN THE UNLIKELY EVENT THAT YOU HAVE TO FIGHT WITH ONE OF YOUR COMRADES, YOU WON'T BE OVERWHELMED.

YOU CAN IMAGINE THE STRENGTH OF THOSE BELOW ME FROM HAVING SEEN ME, NO. 6.
NUMBERS 6 THROUGH 9 ARE ALL ABOUT THE SAME. IF YOU HAD TO TAKE ANY OF THEM ONE ON ONE, YOU SHOULD BE ABLE TO HANDLE THEM.

...

ARE YOU SURE?

YOU'VE GOT TO BE KIDDING.

THE PROBLEM IS NUMBERS 5 AND UP.

TO TELL THE TRUTH, THERE'S A BIG LEAP FROM 5 TO 6.

SHAKAN

GAREK

GAREK

GAREK GAREK

GAREK

THESE ARE THE MARKS OF THE TOP FIVE.
REMEMBER THEM.

FROM THE RIGHT, NO. 5... RAFAELA.
NO. 4... OPHELIA.
NO. 3... GALATEA.
NO. 2... BETH.
NO. 1... ALICIA.

EACH OF THEM IS A MONSTER.
IF YOU MEET ANY OF THEM, AVOID ENGAGING THEM.

READ THIS WAY

GASHAK
GASHAK
GASHAK
GASHAK

READ THIS WAY

SO...
THERE WERE THREE YOMA IN THE VILLAGE ...

...AND YOU FELLED THEM IN AN INSTANT.
EXCEL-LENT.

IT WAS NOTH-ING.
THAT'S MY JOB.

YOUR WORK HAS BEEN COMMEND-ABLE OF LATE.
YOU SEEM TO HAVE STOPPED RUNNING WILD AND SETTLED DOWN.
DID SOME-THING HAPPEN?

NO.
I SUPPOSE AFTER THE RECENT HUNT FOR THE AWAKENED BEING, I CAME TO SEE THE LIMIT OF MY ABILI-TIES.
ONE SMALL MIS-STEP ...
...AND WE WOULD ALL HAVE BEEN DEAD.

SORRY TO KEEP PILING ON THE WORK...
...BUT WE'VE RECEIVED ANOTHER REQUEST ABOUT AN AWAKENED BEING.

READ
THIS
WAY

NORTH OF HERE IS A PLACE CALLED GONAHL ...
...A VILLAGE NEAR A SMALL CASTLE.

IT'S ALREADY IN RUINS.

THE TARGET IS A FORMER SINGLE DIGIT.
THE VILLAGE WAS DESTROYED WITHIN HALF A DAY AFTER SHE ARRIVED.

SHE'S MUCH STRONGER THAN THE MALE YOU FOUGHT BEFORE.
IF YOU DON'T WANT TO DIE, BETTER GIVE IT ALL YOU'VE GOT.

SHAK

I WON'T DIE.

I WON'T.

ZA SHA

READ THIS WAY

GEEZ... WHAT'S GOING ON?
WHAT HAPPENED TO THE VILLAGE?

READ THIS WAY

THIS IS TERRIBLE.
BY THE LOOKS OF THINGS ...
...I'VE GOT A TOUGH BATTLE AHEAD.

THE AURA IS OVER THERE.

LET'S GO, RAKI.
OKAY.

WHAT'S THIS I SENSE?
LIKE SOMETHING STRANGE ... STICKING TO ME.

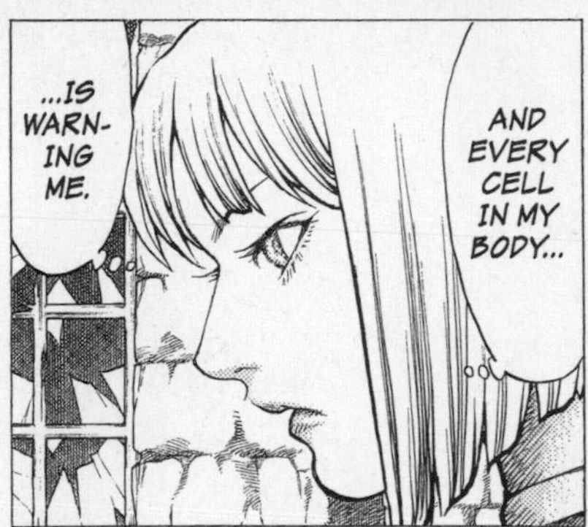
AND EVERY CELL IN MY BODY...
...IS WARNING ME.

KLAK

OH...
HELLO.

SO WHAT'S WITH...
...THE LITTLE BOY?

HIM?
HE'S WITH ME.
THERE WAS NO PLACE NEARBY WHERE I COULD LEAVE HIM, SO I HAD TO BRING HIM ALONG.
IT TOOK US SO LONG TO GET HERE, I THOUGHT THE OTHERS WOULD BE HERE BY NOW.
BUT I GUESS THEY'RE NOT HERE YET.

WHAT ARE YOU TALKING ABOUT? WE'RE BOTH HERE...
...YOU AND ME.
THIS TIME, IT'S THE TWO OF US.
!
JUST TWO?

READ THIS WAY

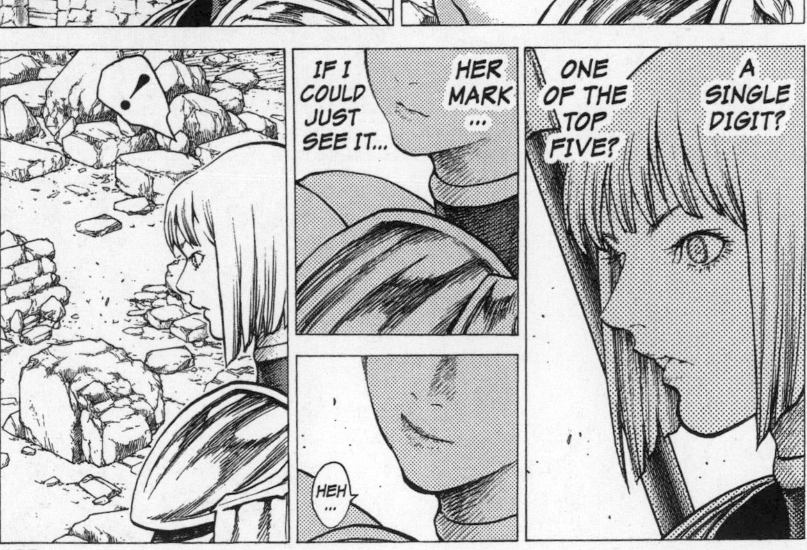

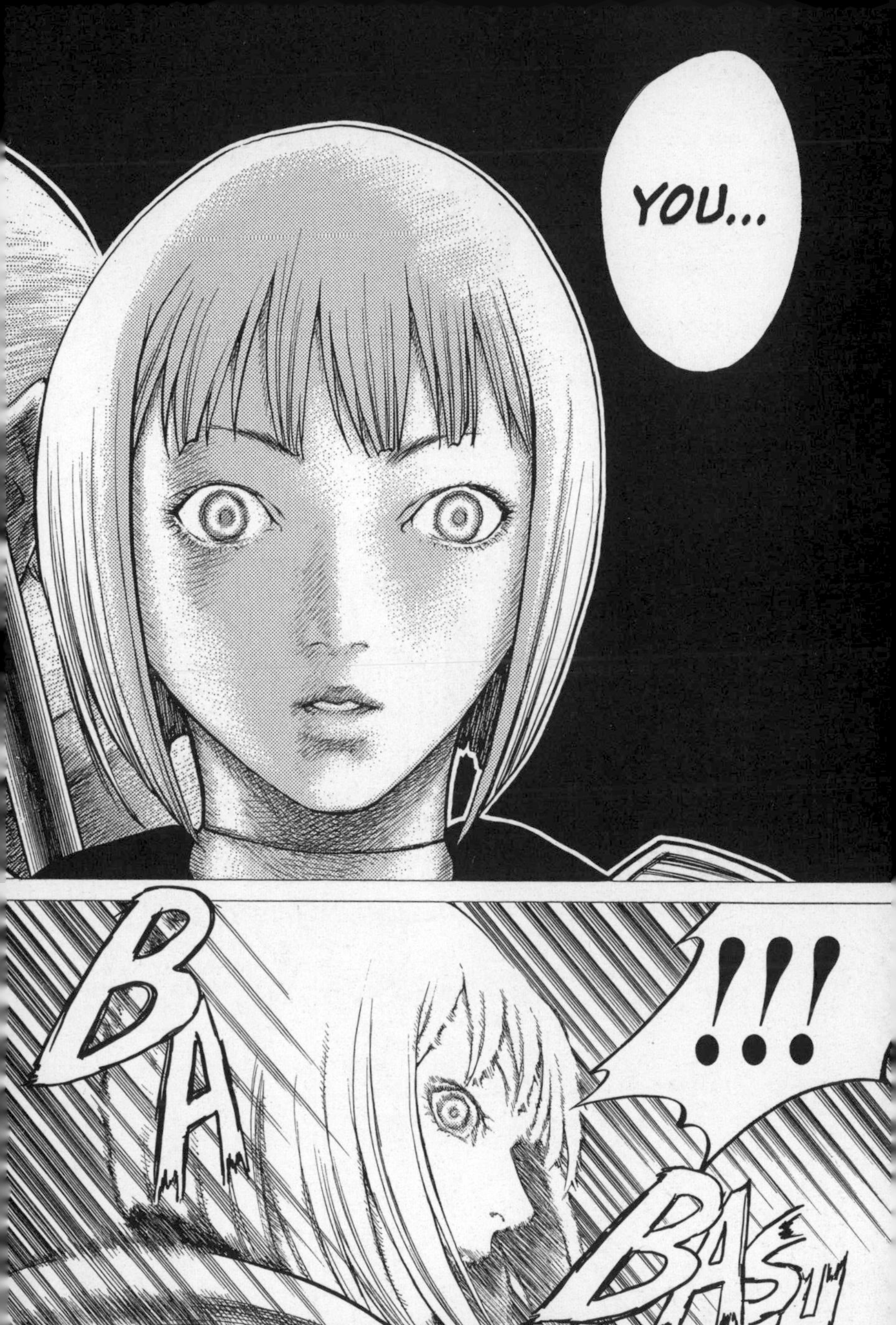
YOU...
!!!
BA
BASH

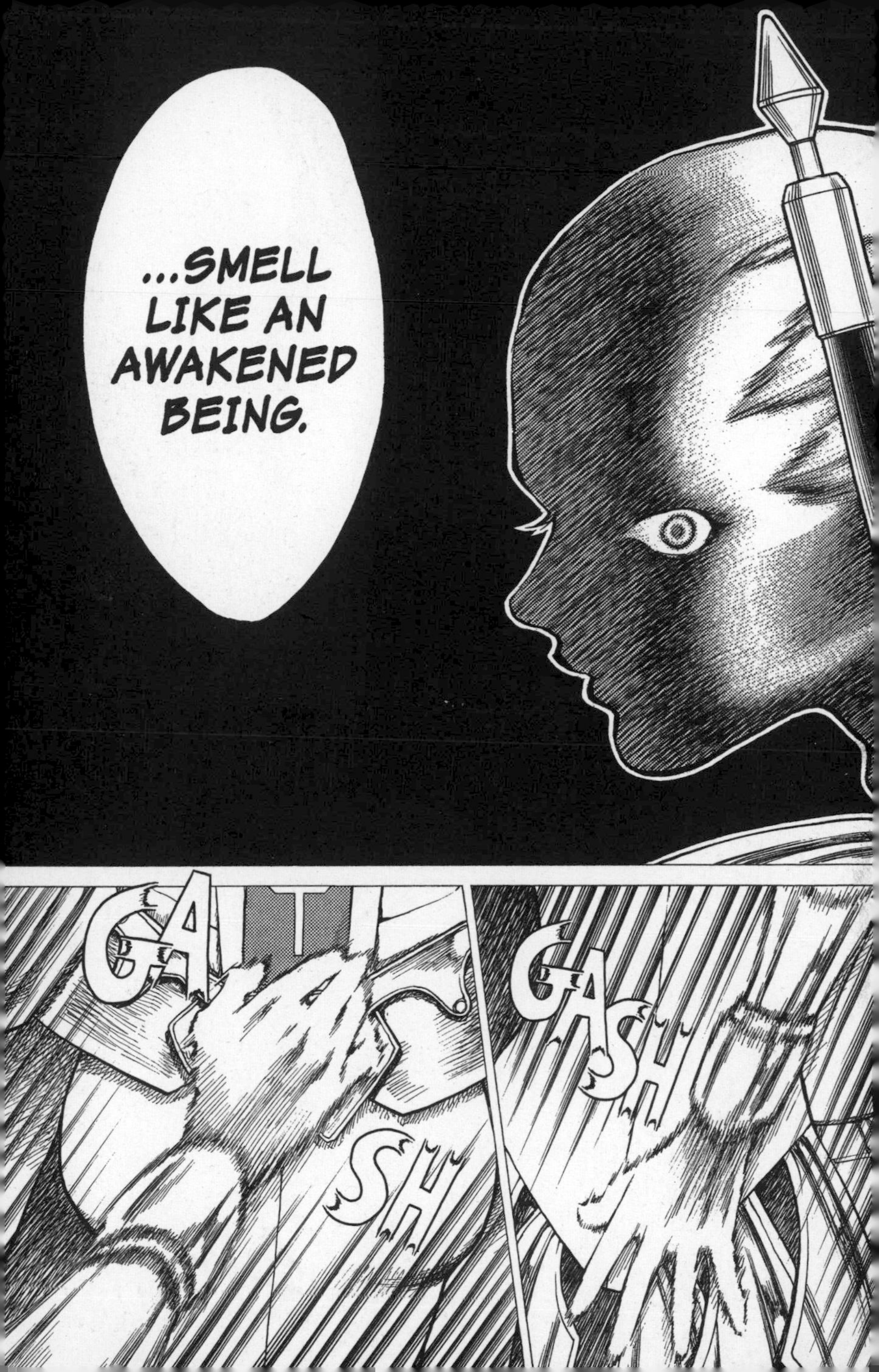

...SMELL LIKE AN AWAKENED BEING.
GASH
GASH

GASH
UH ...
AW... KEEP STILL.
LET ME ENJOY YOUR SCENT.
UH ...
AH ...
I LIKE THAT SMELL.
UH ...
STOP IT, YOU!
GET AWAY FROM CLARE!
GASH
!
DO
SHAK

STAY BACK, BOY...
...OR I'LL KILL YOU!

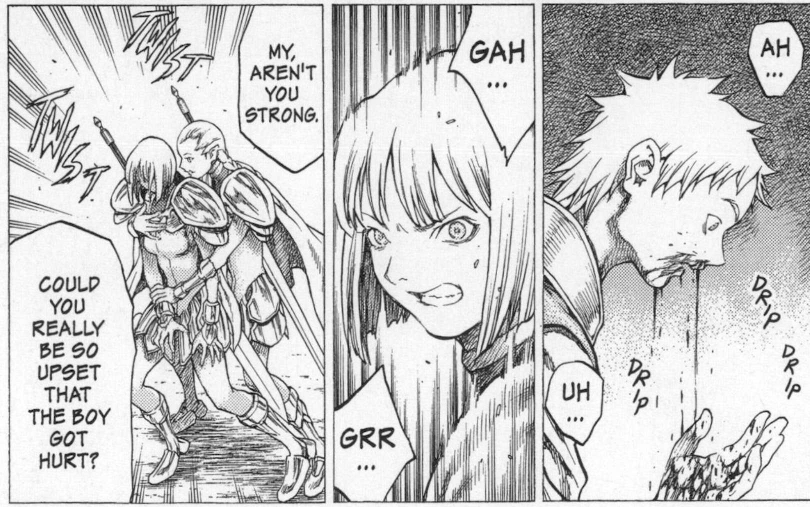

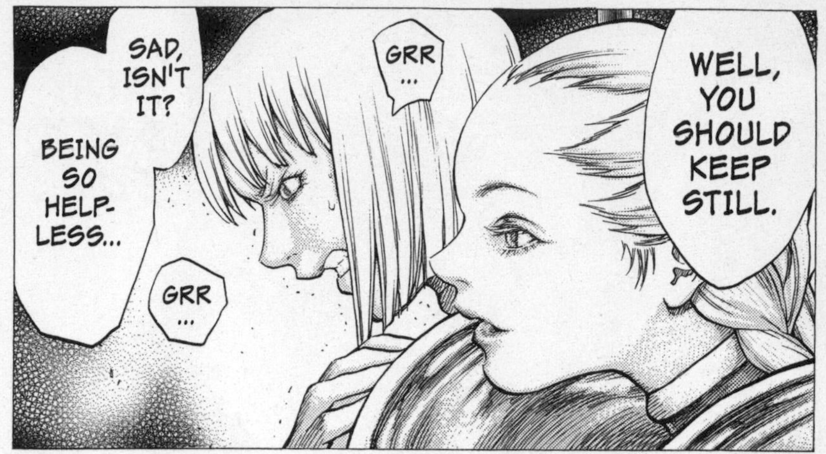
WELL, YOU SHOULD KEEP STILL.
GRR...
SAD, ISN'T IT?
BEING SO HELP-LESS...
GRR...

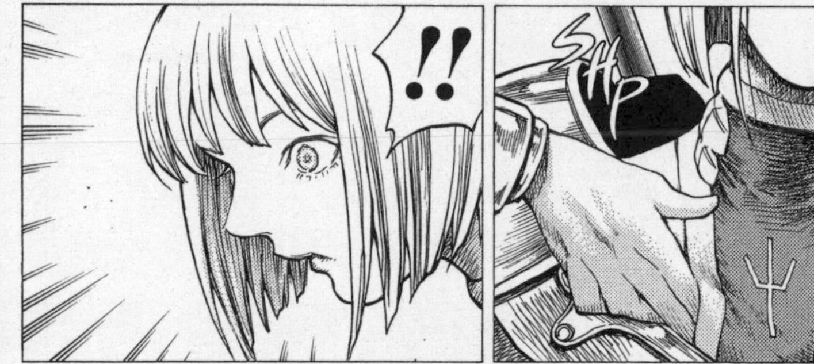
SHP
!!

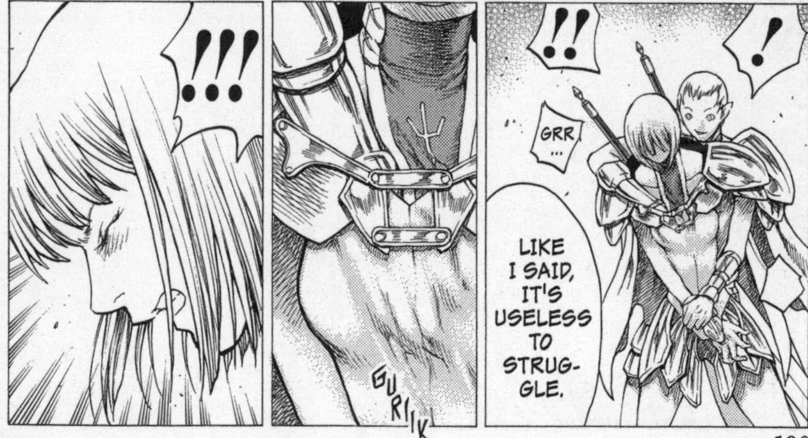
!
!!
GRR...
LIKE I SAID, IT'S USELESS TO STRUG-GLE.
GURIIK
!!!

READ THIS WAY

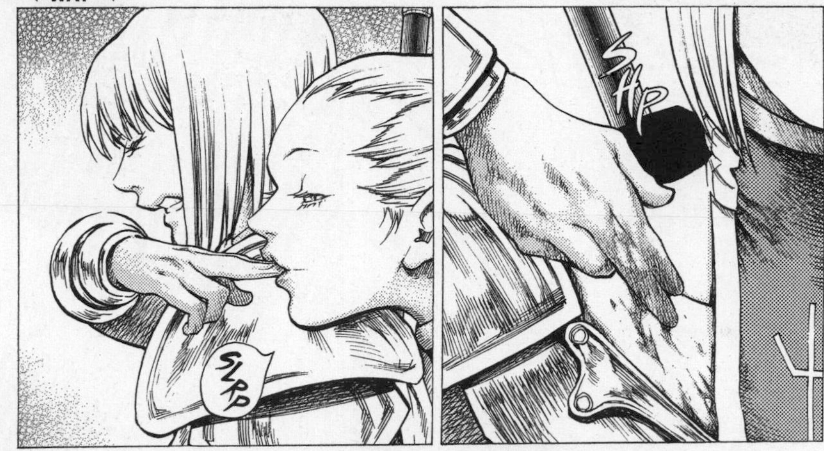
SHP
SLRP

WHAT A STRANGE TASTE.
ARE YOU SURE YOU'RE ONE OF MY COMRADES?

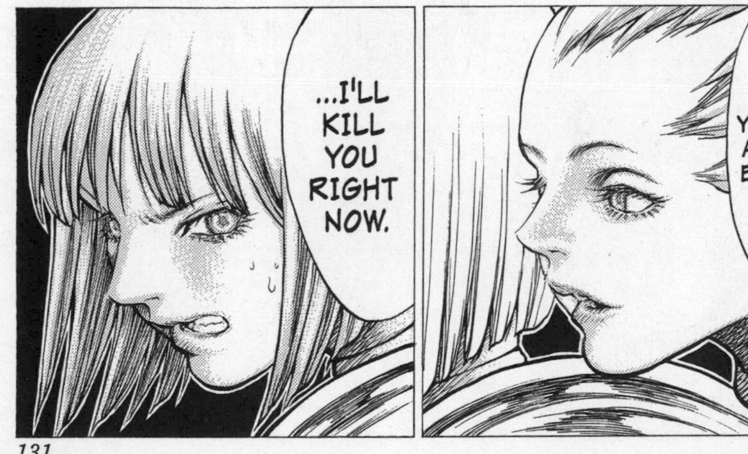
IF YOU'VE AWAK-ENED...
...I'LL KILL YOU RIGHT NOW.

SLASH

SHUP

!!!

SHAKA

RAKI!

HUFF...
HUFF...
HUFF...
HUFF...

HUFF...
IT'S THE SWORD THAT GALK GAVE ME.
TOUCH CLARE AGAIN AND I'LL STICK IT THROUGH YOU.
HUFF...
HUFF...
HUFF...

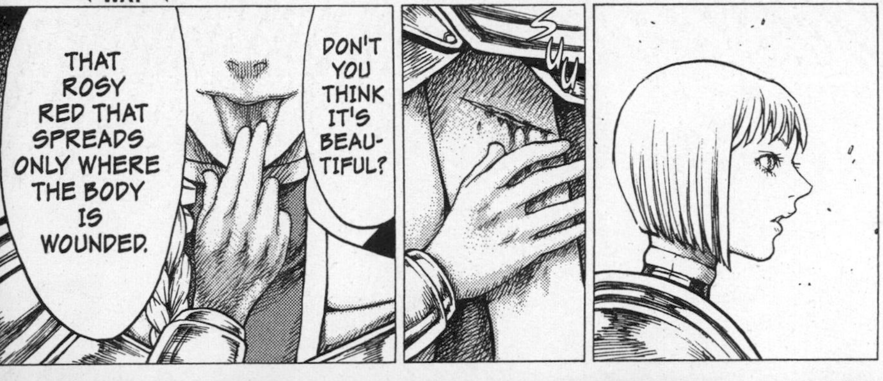

SHALL I PAINT YOU IN THAT LOVELY RED...

...LITTLE BOY?

クレイモア
Claymore™

Scene 32: The Endless Gravestones, Part 2

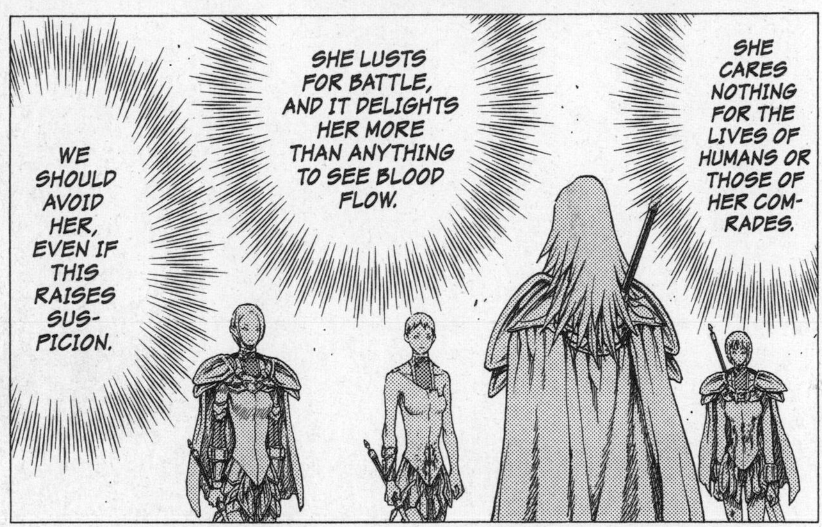

Scene 32: The Endless Gravestones, Part 2
...Ophelia.
The blood-soaked warrior ... No. 4.

READ THIS WAY

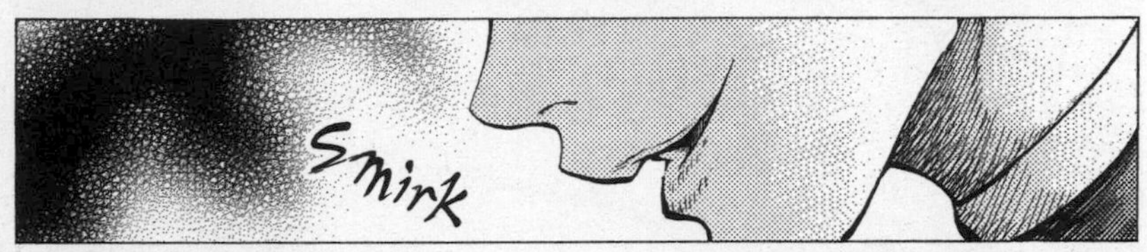
Smirk

WHY ...
YOU TURNED WHITE WHEN YOU SAW MY MARK.
DO YOU KNOW ME?

I WOULDN'T MIND KNOWING...
...HOW YOU HEARD ABOUT ME.
HUFF ...
HUFF ...
HUFF ...

BUT FIRST ...
blink
!

FWASH
GACHA AANG

READ THIS WAY

WHA ...?!
HMPH!

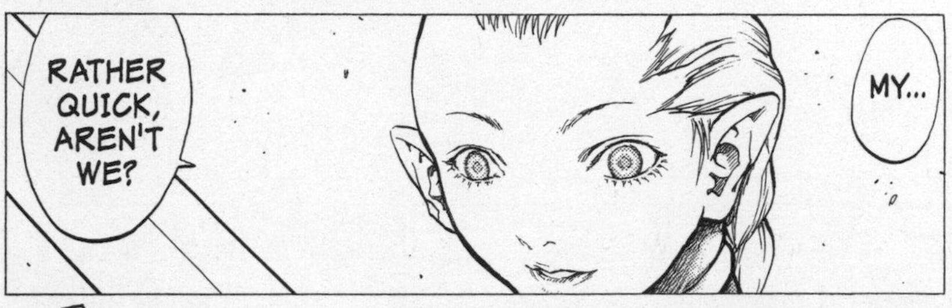
MY...
RATHER QUICK, AREN'T WE?

KAK
FWASH
GACHANG

WHAT—

WHAT ARE YOU DOING?!

THE RULE SAYS THAT IF YOU KILL A HUMAN, YOU FORFEIT YOUR LIFE.

YOU WERE ABOUT TO KILL THIS BOY.

DO YOU WANT TO DIE?

YOU'RE ALL SUCH FOOLS.

THAT WOULD ONLY HAPPEN IF YOU REPORTED YOURSELF.

IT'S YOUR NECK ON THE LINE, YET YOU FEEL OBLIGED TO BE TRUTHFUL. WHAT'S WRONG WITH YOU?

WELL, EVEN IF THERE WERE WITNESSES...

...THE MATTER WOULD BE FINISHED ONCE I GOT RID OF THEM.

THWOK

DOSHAAK

CLARE!

READ
THIS
WAY

LISTEN ...
I'LL EXPLAIN THE RULES.

FROM HERE ON, I'LL FIGHT THE BOY.
NOT FOR REAL, OF COURSE. I'LL JUST MATCH HIS STRENGTH.
AGH ...
BUT WITH EACH PASSING MINUTE, I'LL INCREASE MY SPEED AND STRENGTH.
AH ...
GA ...
MY GUESS IS HE WON'T LAST MORE THAN TEN MINUTES, HOWEVER HARD HE FIGHTS.

YOU'LL HAVE TO REATTACH YOUR LEGS BEFORE THEN AND SAVE HIM.
TAKE TOO LONG, AND HE DIES. RUSH, AND YOU'LL FAIL. YOU'LL BE USELESS TO HIM. DOESN'T IT SOUND FUN?
AGH ...
AH ...
GA ...

ARE YOU ...
...READY?
LET'S GO!
GACHANG
!!
ARGH!
KLANG
KLANG
KLANG
KLANG
UCK!
UGH!
KLANG
KLANG
KLANG
KLANG
KLANG

READ THIS WAY

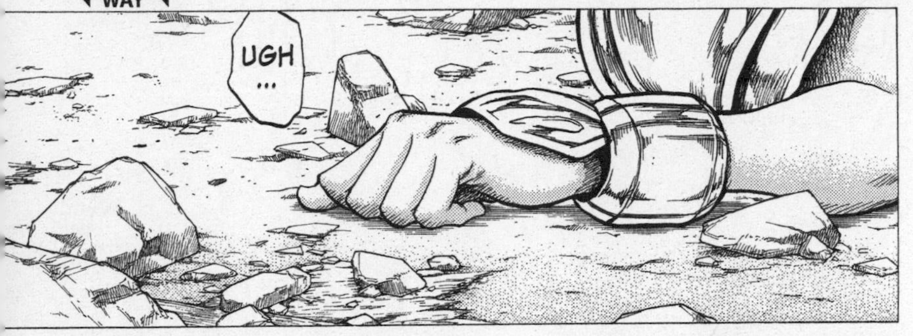

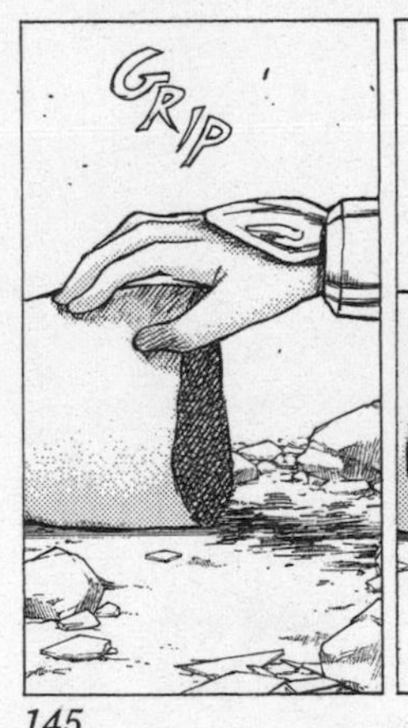

SHAP
BAM
BIKI
BIKI
BIKI
BIKI
BIKI
STAY CALM... STAY CALM.
I SHOULD BE ABLE TO DO THIS BY RELEASING MY POWER AND FOCUSING ON REGENERATING.
JUST RELAX AND STAY CALM.
BIKI
HEH...
!
SWOOK
GAH!

MY, MY.
KLANG
KLANG
YOU'RE BETTER THAN I THOUGHT.
I'M ALMOST IM-PRESSED.
KLANG
IT'S A LITTLE EARLY...
...BUT LET'S TAKE IT UP A NOTCH.
SHUP
KLANG
!!
UH ...

AGH!
RAKI!
AUGH!
HOLD YOUR SWORD UP PROPERLY.
IT'S A DOUBLE-EDGED BLADE, SO ONE EDGE IS FACING YOU, TOO.
KLANG
KLAK
KLAK
DAMN IT!
DAMN IT!
BIKI
BIKI BIKI
OH MY.
KLAK
KLAK
NOT WORKING, IS IT?
KLAK
KLANG

READ THIS WAY

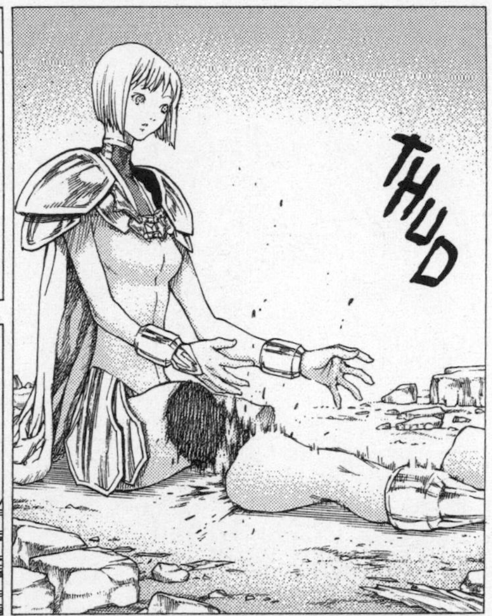

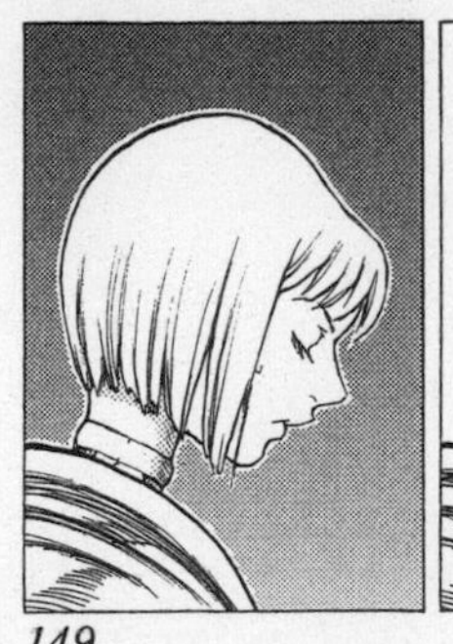

BIKI

BIKI

BIKI

BIKI

BIKI

VREEEN

SHE REACTED JUST THE WAY I WANTED.

SUCH AN OBEDIENT CHILD.

HEH...

HUFF ...
HUFF ...
HUFF ...

SLASH
!
SLASH
!!

THERE!
AND THERE!
SLASH
SLASH

MY, MY!
!

HUFF ...
HUFF ...
HUFF ...

BABAM

HA HA
HA HA
HA HA
HA HA
HA HA
HA HA
HA HA
HA HA
HA HA
HA HA!

HA HA
HA HA!
FASCIN-
ATING!

BAM

HE'S
TOO
MUCH!

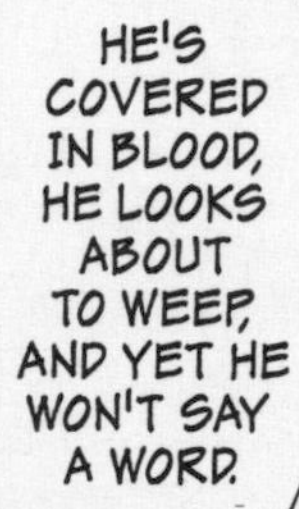

READ THIS WAY

KEEP IT TO YOURSELF, WHY DON'T YOU! YOUR ATTACKS ARE USELESS!
YOUR MEASLY BLOWS AREN'T EVEN MAKING A SCRATCH!

SHIVER

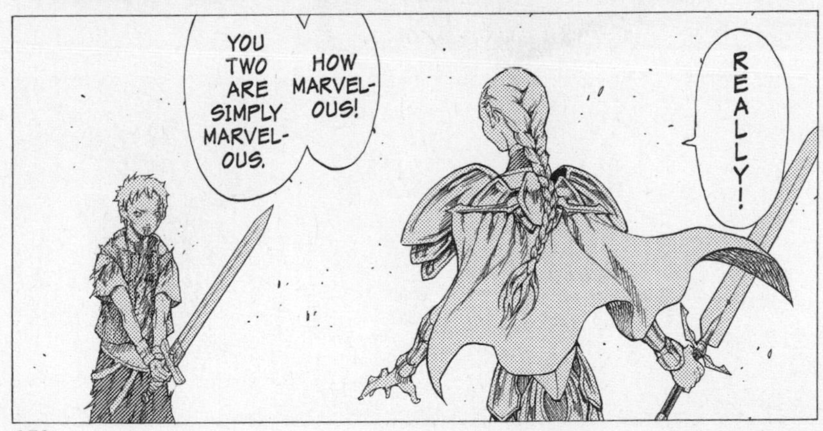
REALLY!
HOW MARVELOUS!
YOU TWO ARE SIMPLY MARVELOUS.

WHICH ONE OF YOU SHOULD I KILL?

WHICH OF YOU WOULD BE MORE FUN TO WATCH AS YOU WAIL IN AGONY?

READ THIS WAY

OH...
WHAT ARE YOU ALL DOING HERE?

STOP! DON'T COME NEAR US!
RUN AWAY!

RUN AWAY?
BUT WHY?

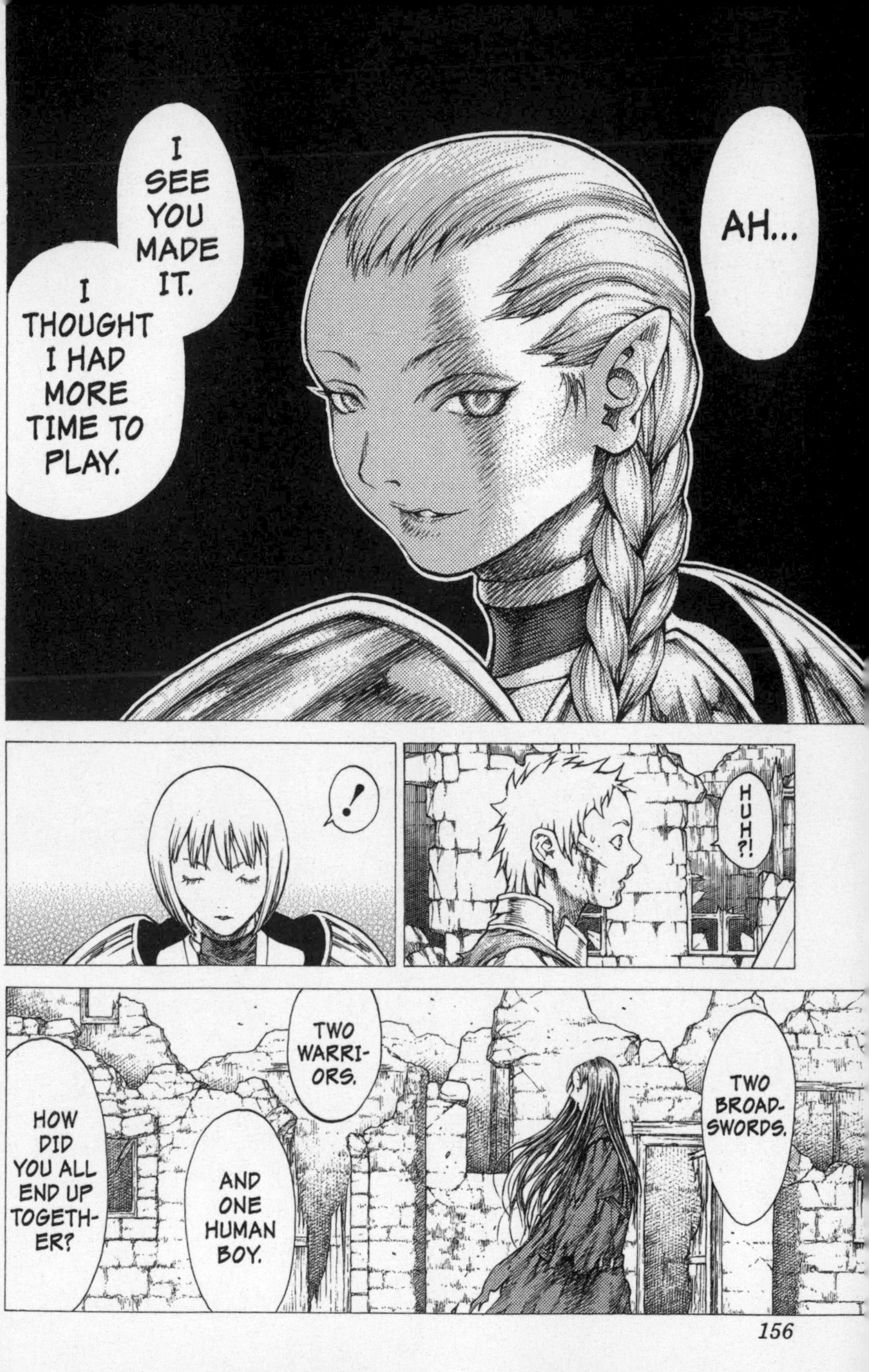

AH...
I SEE YOU MADE IT.
I THOUGHT I HAD MORE TIME TO PLAY.
HUH?!
!
TWO BROADSWORDS.
TWO WARRIORS.
AND ONE HUMAN BOY.
HOW DID YOU ALL END UP TOGETHER?

...BUT THE BOY...

...SMELLS SO DELICIOUS, HE'S IRRESISTIBLE.

BOKO

BAKI BAKI

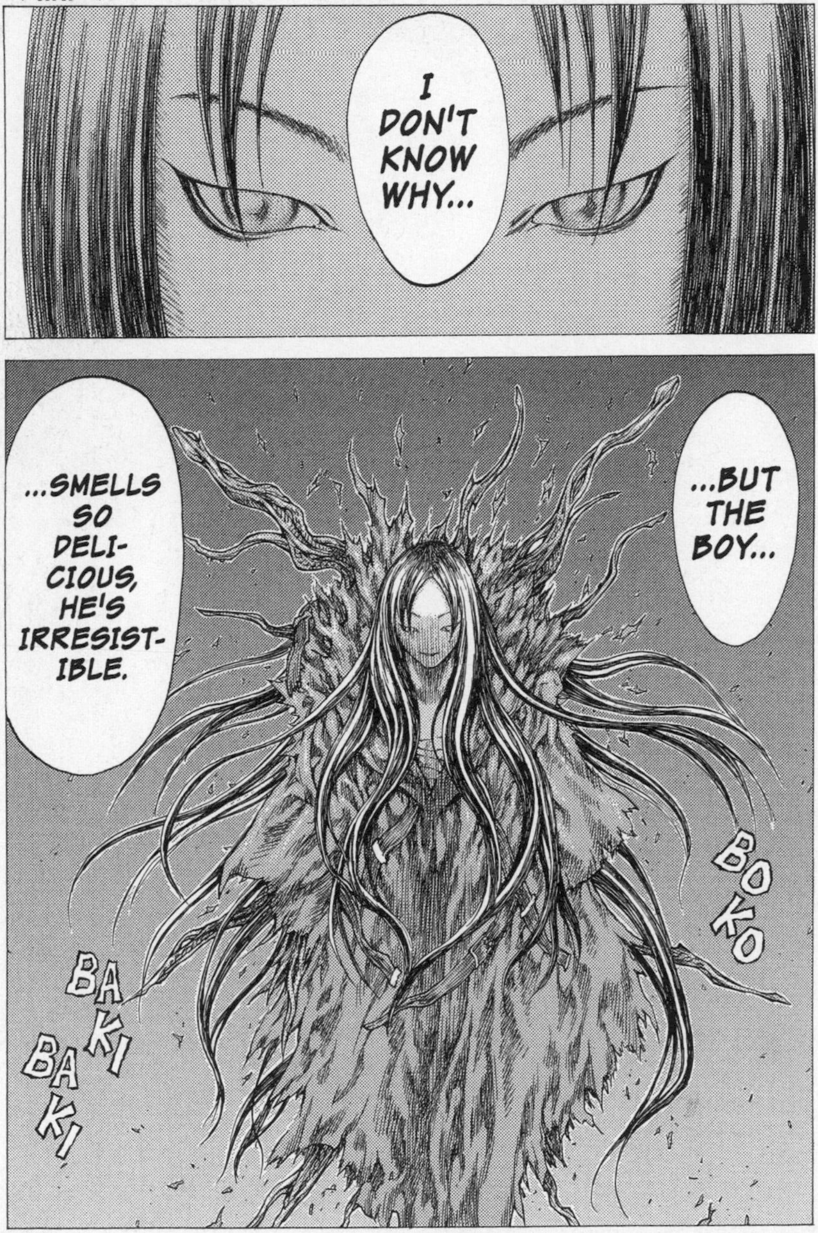

クレイモア
Claymore™

Scene 33: The Endless Gravestones, Part 3

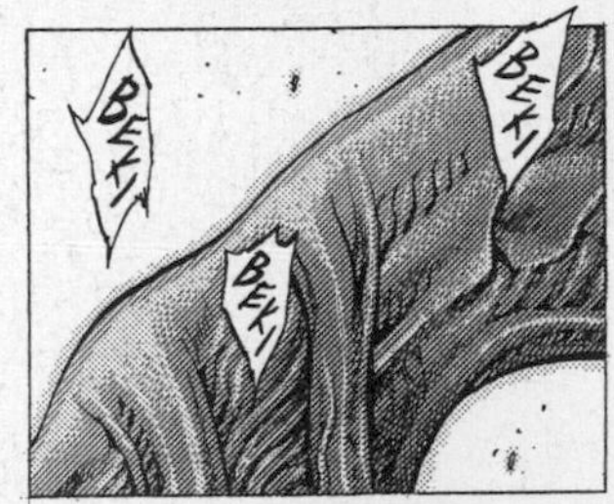

Scene 33: The Endless Gravestones, Part 3

IT'S ...
...A MONSTER!

WELL, WELL.
THIS ONE LOOKS PRETTY STRONG.

I WONDER IF...
... WE'LL DEFEAT IT.
UGH!
PASH
GASHAP

BIKI
BIKI
BIKI
BIKI
HYUUUU
BIKI
BIKI
BIKI

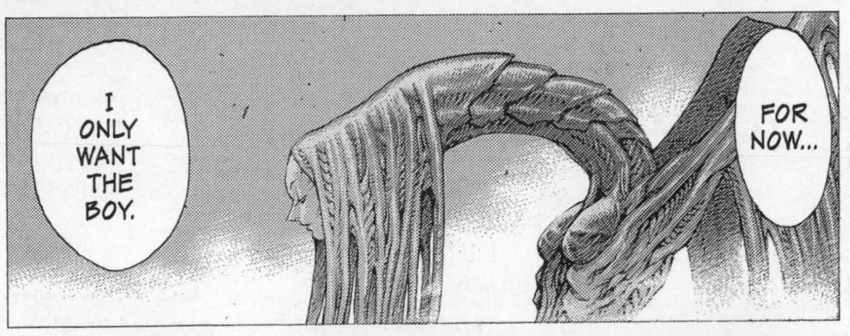

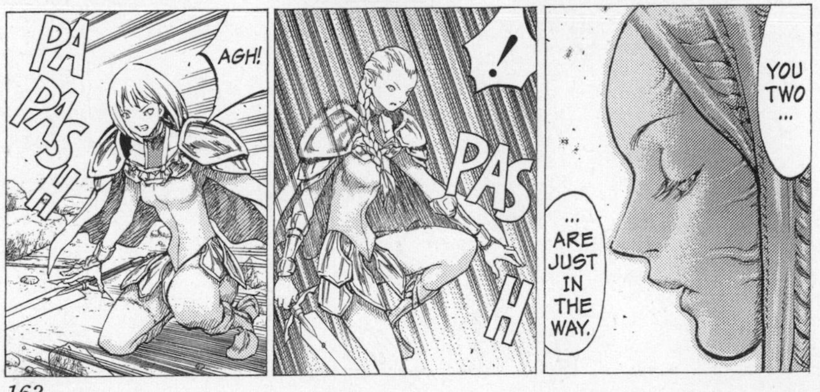

DAGAAA
DAGAGAGAGAGA
DAKAA
DABAAA

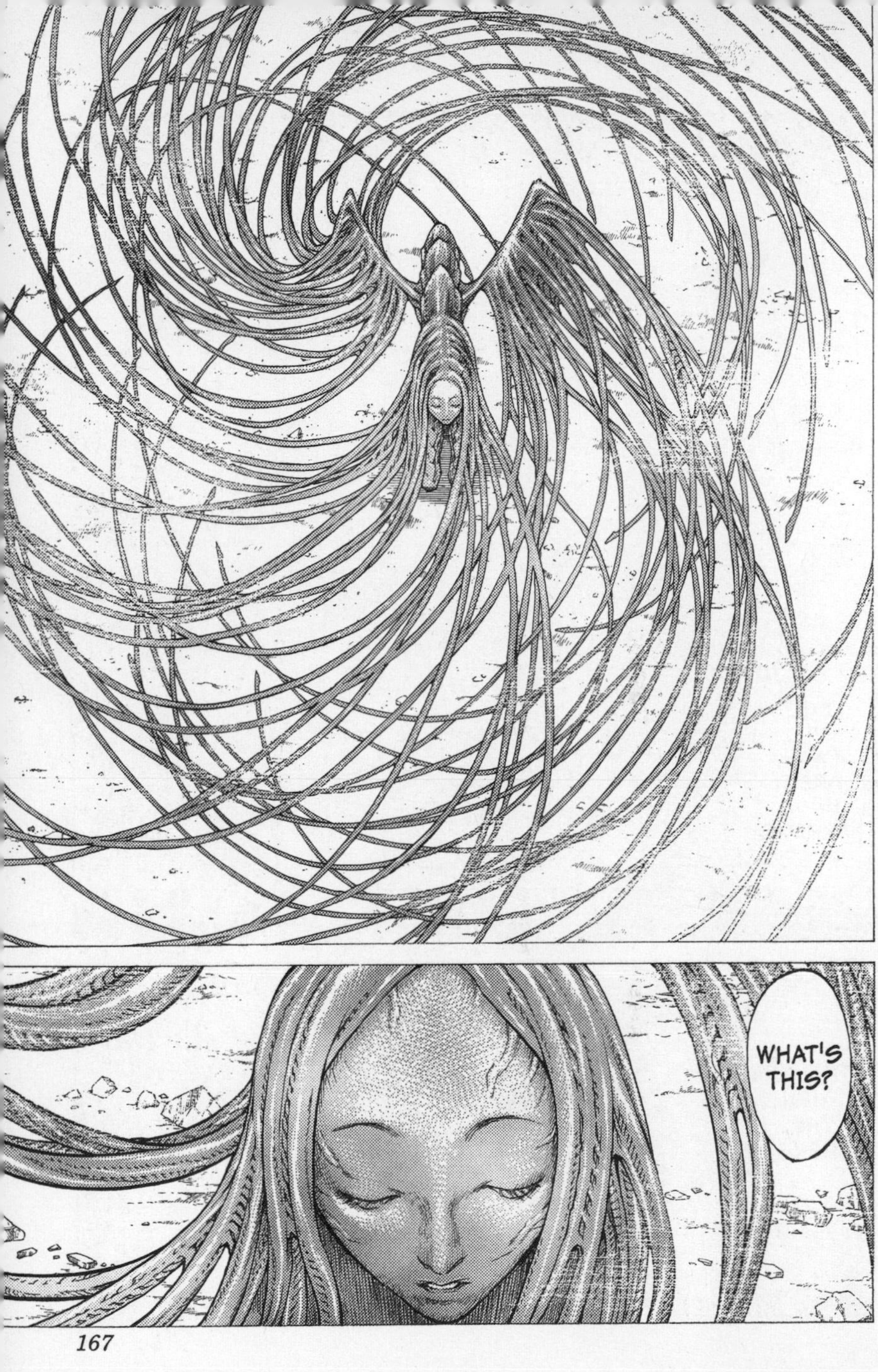

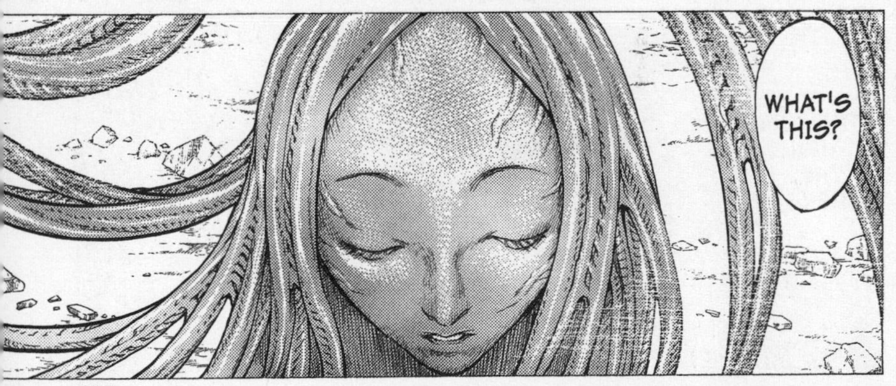
WHAT'S THIS?

I MEANT TO CRUSH EVERY-THING BUT THE BOY...
...BUT YOU TWO ARE UN-HARMED.

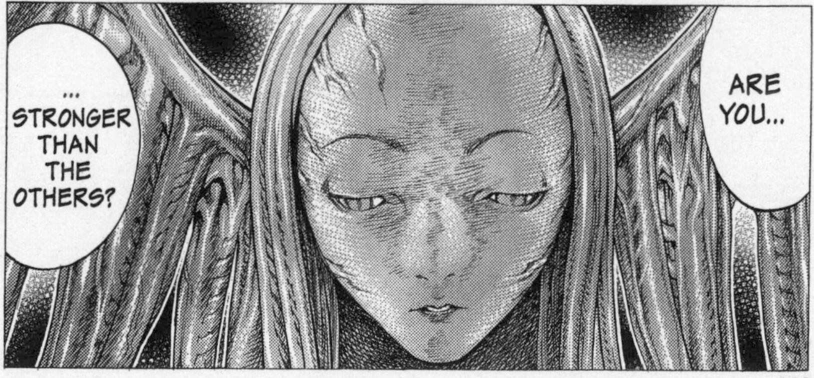
ARE YOU...
... STRONGER THAN THE OTHERS?

READ THIS WAY

WHAM
!
!!
BAM

GRAB
AH!
RAKI!

LEAVE THE BOY TO ME!
HURRY UP AND ATTACH YOUR LEG!

WE'VE GOT TO MOVE FAST!
YOU SAW HOW STRONG THAT THING IS!

THIS IS NO TIME TO ARGUE!

...

UGH ...
GASH

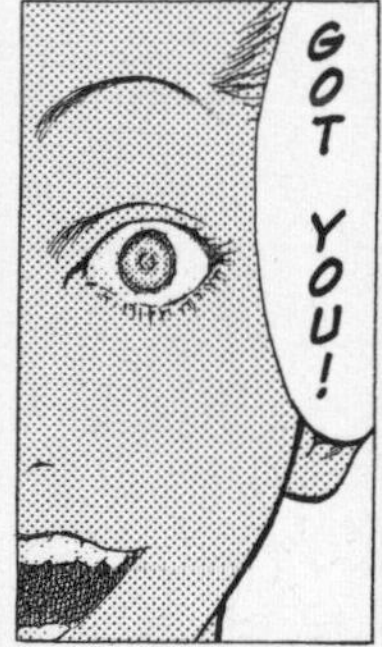
GOT YOU!

!!!
FWASH
AH!
SHWUP
FWOOP

RAKI!!

WHAM
SHP

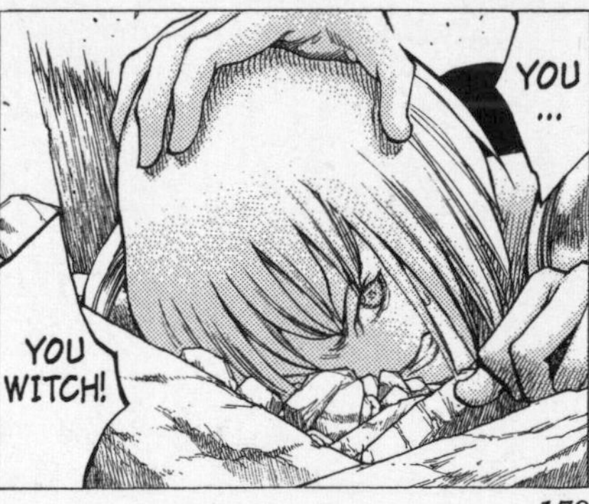
YOU ...
YOU WITCH!

SORRY.
MY HANDS SLIPPED.

UH ...
AH ...
WHY YOU ...!
LEMME GO, YOU MON-STER!

BIKI

BOKO

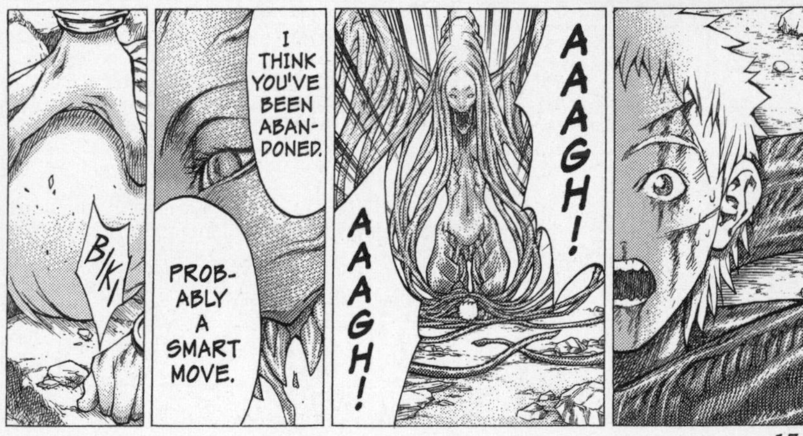
BIKI
I THINK YOU'VE BEEN ABANDONED.
PROBABLY A SMART MOVE.
AAAAGH!
AAAAGH!

VWOOM
!

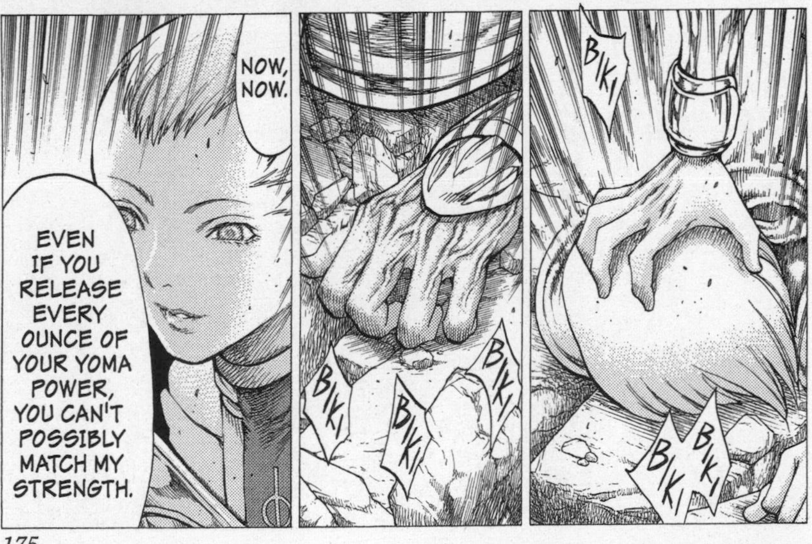

BIKI
BIKI
BIKI
BIKI
BIKI
BIKI
BIKI
NOW, NOW.
EVEN IF YOU RELEASE EVERY OUNCE OF YOUR YOMA POWER, YOU CAN'T POSSIBLY MATCH MY STRENGTH.

AAH!
AAAAH!

GUH!
GUH!
GUH!
BIKI
BIKI
BIKI
BIKI

...YOU MONSTER!
STAY BACK...

BIKI
BIKI
BIKI
BIKI

AGH!

DON'T BE A SORE LOSER.
BIKI
BETTER GIVE UP ON HIM.
YOU CAN'T HELP HIM, NO MATTER HOW MUCH YOMA POWER YOU RELEASE.
BESIDES...
...YOUR MISERABLE POWER COULDN'T SAVE ANYONE.
BIKI
BIKI
BIKI

VWO
OM

AASH
!
GAH!

FWA

BWA HA HA HA!
HA HA!
YOU WENT AND *DID* IT!

THE BLOOD WENT RUSHING TO THAT THICK HEAD OF YOURS, AND YOU WENT BEYOND YOUR LIMITS!
YOU AWAKENED TO SAVE THE BOY...
...BUT NOW YOU CAN'T HELP HIM AT ALL, YOU FOOL!

HUH?

READ THIS WAY

WHAT...

YOU ...

YOU MUST BE BEYOND YOUR LIMITS NOW.
ARE YOU CHEAT -ING?

AND BOTH YOUR LEGS ARE FIRMLY ATTACHED.
YET...
ONCE YOU PASS YOUR LIMITS, THERE'S NO TURNING BACK.

AH!
SNAP

THAT MUST MEAN...
... YOU'VE AWAK-ENED.

?

INTER-ESTING ...
VERY INTER-ESTING.

IN JUST ONE DAY...
...I'LL GET TO KILL TWO AWAKENED BEINGS!

BA-BUMP
BA-BUMP
BA-BUMP

GRIP

TIGHTER!
WITH ALL YOUR STRENGTH!

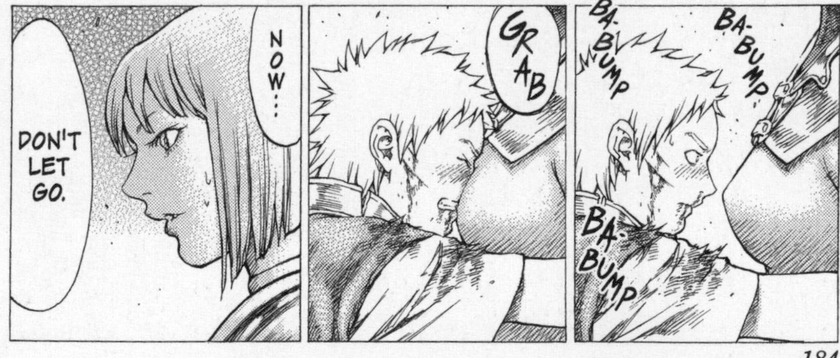
BA-BUMP
BA-BUMP
BA-BUMP
GRAB
NOW...
DON'T LET GO.

DOM

!!

DO
GA
GA
GA

SHP

DID YOU BLOCK THEM ALL?
YOU'RE QUITE GOOD.

READ THIS WAY

YOU SAID SOME-THING INTER-ESTING BEFORE ...
...ABOUT KILLING ME.

I COULD PROBABLY CATCH THOSE CHILDREN EASILY...
...BUT I THINK I'LL START BY EATING YOUR ARROGANT LITTLE HEART.

...

SHH

HEH!
PASH

DON'T BE SO CON- CEITED ...
...YOU MON- STROUS BITCH!

End of Vol. 6: The Endless Gravestones

IN THE NEXT VOLUME

Ophelia turns out to be even more of a monster than the Awakened Being that destroyed the village. She hunts Clare down, using her heightened Yoma powers, and the two begin a battle to the death.

Available Now

You're Reading in the Wrong Direction!!

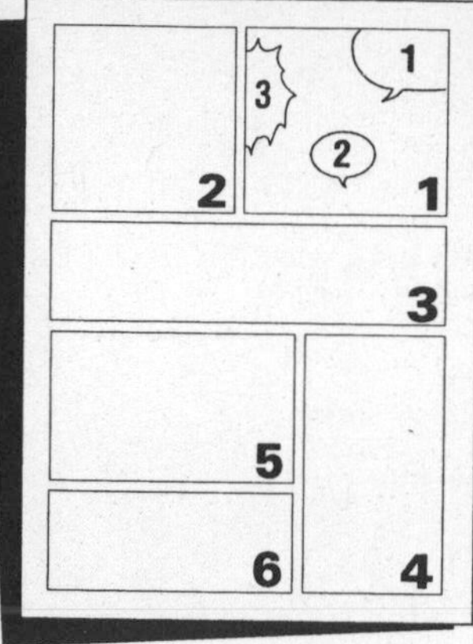

Whoops! Guess what? You're starting at the wrong end of the comic!

...It's true! In keeping with the original Japanese format, **Claymore** is meant to be read from right to left, starting in the upper-right corner.

Unlike English, which is read from left to right, Japanese is read from right to left, meaning that action, sound effects and word-balloon order are completely reversed... something which can make readers unfamiliar with Japanese feel pretty backwards themselves. For this reason, manga or Japanese comics published in the U.S. in English have sometimes been published "flopped"—that is, printed in exact reverse order, as though seen from the other side of a mirror.

By flopping pages, U.S. publishers can avoid confusing readers, but the compromise is not without its downside. For one thing, a character in a flopped manga series who once wore in the original Japanese version a T-shirt emblazoned with "M A Y" (as in "the merry month of") now wears one which reads "Y A M"! Additionally, many manga creators in Japan are themselves unhappy with the process, as some feel the mirror-imaging of their art skews their original intentions.

We are proud to bring you Norihiro Yagi's **Claymore** in the original unflopped format. For now, though, turn to the other side of the book and let the adventure begin...!

—Editor